IW 8 6

£1.50

A WORDSWORTH COLOUR GUIDE

CIVIL
AIRCRAFT

Wordsworth Editions

First published in England 1993 by
Wordsworth Editions Ltd
Cumberland House
Crib Street
Ware
Hertfordshire SG12 9ET

ISBN 1 85326 989 1

Photographs by courtesy of TRH Pictures London

Set in 8½/9pt Monophoto Univers
Text conversion and pagination by
August Filmsetting, St Helens

Printed in Italy by Amadeus s.p.a.

Contents

Aérospatiale (Sud Aviation) Caravelle

Country of origin: France
First flight: May 1955
Entered airline service: May 1959 with Air France
Production: 280 built; 63 in service
Powerplant: two 5,725kgp (12,600lb st) Rolls-Royce Avon 532R or 533R turbojets
Performance: maximum cruising speed 845km/h (525mph) at 7,620m (25,000ft); range with maximum payload 2,300km (1,430 miles)
Weights: basic operating 28,655kg (63,175lb); maximum payload 8,200kg (18,080lb); maximum take-off 50,000kg (110,230lb)
Dimensions: span 34.3m (112ft 7in); length 32.01m (105ft); height 8.72m (28ft 7in); wing area 146.7m² (1,579sq ft)
Seating capacity: 64
History: the Caravelle was the world's third jet-powered airliner to enter service and the first with engines pod-mounted on the sides of the rear fuselage to reduce cabin noise. In total, nine versions were built, culminating in the Caravelle 12, which was powered by two 6,577kgp (14,500lb st) thrust Pratt & Whitney JT8D-9 turbofans.

France's first jet-powered airliner successfully evolved into the Super Caravelle

Aérospatiale Corvette 100

Country of origin: France
First flight: July 1970
Entered service: Sept 1974 with Air Alps
Production: 40 built; 30 in service
Powerplant: two 1,048kgp (2,310lb st) Pratt & Whitney (VALL) JT15D-4 turbofans
Performance: maximum cruising speed 796km/h (495 mph) at 9,145m (30,000ft); best economy cruise 630km/h (391mph) at 11,000m (36,100ft); initial rate of climb 15.25m/sec (3,000ft/min); service ceiling 11,580m (38,000ft); range with maximum payload 1,645km (1,022 miles); range with maximum fuel 2,690km (1,670 miles)
Weights: empty equipped 3,622kg (7,985lb); maximum payload 1,020kg (2,248lb); maximum take-off 6,100kg (13,450lb)
Dimensions: span 12.8m (42ft); length 13.82m (45ft 4in); height 4.23m (13ft 10in); wing area 22m² (236.8sq ft)
Seating capacity: 12
History: the first production aircraft flew on 9 November 1973, because deliveries were seriously delayed by strikes at the Canadian plant manufacturing the Pratt & Whitney engines. Extended range was achieved by the use of wingtip tanks, and plans to develop a stretched fuselage variant, the 200, were cancelled.

The Aérospatiale Corvette 100, which
6 *met with very limited success*

Aérospatiale/British Aerospace Concorde

Country of origin: France/UK
First flight: 001, March 1969; 002, April 1969
Entered service: January 1976 with British Airways and Air France
Production: 16 built; 14 in service
Powerplant: four 17,260kgp (38,050lb st) Rolls-Royce/SNECMA Olympus 593 Mk 610 turbojets with silencers and reversers
Performance: maximum cruising speed 2,333km/h (1,450mph) at 16,600m (54,500ft); best range cruise, Mach 2.5; service ceiling about 18,288m (60,000ft); range with maximum payload 4,900km (3,050 miles); range with maximum fuel 7,215km (4,490 miles)
Weights: maximum take-off 181,400kg (400,000lb); maximum landing 108,860kg (240,000lb)
Dimensions: span 25.6m (85ft); length 62.17m (203ft 11.5in); height 12.19m (40ft); wing area 358.25m² (3,856sq ft)
Seating capacity: 128
History: the Supersonic Transport Aircraft Committee was established in 1956, and France joined in the project on 29 November 1962; since then all production has alternated on two lines, at Toulouse and Filton. Transatlantic flights from London and Paris to Washington (Dulles) began in May 1976, and to New York in December 1977.

Airbus Industrie A300 B2

Country of origin: European
First flight: 1972
Entered service: 1974 with Air France
Production: 74 on order; 331 in service
Powerplant: two General Electric CF6-50A turbofans rated at 23,133kgp (51,000lb st)
Performance: maximum operating speed 666km/h (413mph); range with maximum payload 1,668km (1,035 miles); range with maximum fuel 3,700km (2,300 miles)
Weights: operating empty 84,810kg (186,980lb); maximum structural payload 31,690kg (69,850lb); maximum usable fuel 34,500kg (76,000lb); maximum take-off 142,000kg (313,055lb); maximum landing weight 130,000kg (286,600lb); maximum zero-fuel weight 120,500kg (265,655lb)
Dimensions: span 44.84m (147ft 1in); length 53.62m (175ft 11in); height 16.53m (54ft 2in); wing area 260m² (2,800sq ft)
Seating capacity: 281
History: a 'wide body' short-to-medium range airliner, of which the A300-600 is the most advanced version, accommodating up to 344 passengers, it incorporates wingtip fences and is available with a choice of General Electric CF6, Pratt & Whitney PW 4158 or Rolls-Royce RB.211 turbofans.

The A300 B2 was the initial production model

Airbus Industrie A310-202

Country of origin: European
Entered service: April 1983 with Swissair
Production: 69 on order; 176 in service
Powerplant: two General Electric CF6-80A turbofans of 21,800kgp (48,000lb st) each; fuel capacity 43,039kg (94,800lb)
Performance: cruising speed Mach 0.78 at 10,670m (35,000ft), ISA; take-off field length, maximum weight, 1,981m (6,500ft); approach speed at maximum landing weight 246km/h (133mph); range with 234 passengers and baggage 4,815km (2,600 naut miles); range with maximum payload 1,870km (1,550 naut miles)
Weights: maximum payload 32,400kg (71,500lb); maximum take-off 132,000kg (291,010lb); maximum landing 118,500kg (261,250lb)
Dimensions: span 43.9m (144ft); length 46.66m (153ft 1in); height 15.8m (51ft 10in); wing area 219m² (2,350sq ft)
Seating capacity: 214
History: designed with a shorter fuselage than the A300, the A310 also incorporated a new wing design and smaller tail plane. The A310-300 longer-range version seats up to 280 passengers.

The A310-200s had wing-tip fences fitted retrospectively after their successful application to the A310-300

Airbus Industrie A320-200

Country of origin: European
First flight: February 1987
Production: number on order, 533; in airline service, 117
Powerplant: two 11,340kgp (25,000lb st) General Electric/SNECMA CFM 56-5 or IAE V2500 turbofans
Performance: maximum speed 903km/h (560mph) at 8,535m (28,000ft); operational ceiling 13,000 + m (42,650 + ft); range 4,730km (2,940 miles) with maximum payload
Weights: empty 39,268kg (86,570lb); maximum take-off 71,986kg (158,700lb:); payload up to 19,142kg (42,200lb) including belly cargo
Dimensions: span 33.91m (111ft 3in); length 37.58m (123ft 3in); wing area 122.4m² (1,318sq ft)
Seating capacity: up to 164 in single-class cabin
History: the A320 is a wholly new design, using a high percentage of composite materials and advanced electronic features including a digital fly-by-wire flight control system with sidestick controllers, an electronic flight instrument system and an electronic centralised aircraft monitor. The Airbus consortium companies are France, Germany, Spain and the UK.

The A320 entered service in March 1988, following an accelerated flight test and certification programme

14

Airbus Industrie A330

Country of origin: European
First flight: 1992
Production: number on order, 121
Powerplant: two General Electric CF6 turbofans, each rated at 29,030kgp (64,000lb st) for take-off or two Pratt & Whitney PW4000 turbofans, each rated at 27,216kgp (60,000lb st) for take-off, with thrust reversers; fuel capacity 111,380 litres (24,500 Imp gal)
Performance: design range about 9,300km (5,000 naut miles) with typical two-class passenger payload
Weights: empty 111,130kg (145,000lb); maximum take-off 204,000kg (450,000lb)
Dimensions: span with wingtip fences 58m (190ft); overall length 62.6m (205ft 4.5in); overall height 16.8m (55ft 1.5in); wing area 325m² (3,500sq ft)
Accommodation: 335 in two-class layout
History: the A330 and A340 are designed to use the same fuselage cross-section as the A300 and A310, with a new and longer centre section to mate with a new wing, thus providing an extra 5.2m (17ft) of additional seating capacity. The new wing will be common to both the A330 and A340, with the ability to accommodate either two or four engines.

An Airbus A330 prototype testing flight

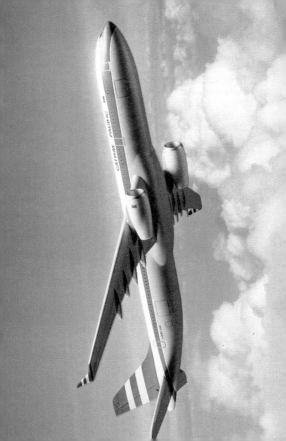

Airbus Industrie A340-200

Country of origin: European
First flight: 1991
Production: number on order, 86
Powerplant: four CFM International CFM 56-5S3 turbofans, each rated at 13,880kgp (30,600lb st) for take-off with thrust reversers
Performance: design range about 14,200km (7,650 naut miles) with typical full three-class passenger payload
Weights: empty 111,130kg (145,000lb); maximum take-off 246,000kg (542,300lb)
Dimensions: span with wingtip fences 58m (190ft); overall length 59.38m (194ft 10in); overall height 16.8m (55ft 1.5in); wing area 325.2m² (3,500sq ft)
Seating capacity: 262 in three-class layout; maximum single-class seating 375
History: a four-engined version of the A330 using common fuselage, wing and tail units. Cockpit and systems are based on those of the A320 with fly-by-wire controls, side-stick controllers and digital integrated displays.

The Airbus A340 has now entered airline service

Antonov An-72 'Coaler'

Country of origin: USSR
Entered service: December 1977 with Aeroflot
Production: figures not available
Powerplant: two 6,500kgp (14,330lb) Lotarev D-36 high-bypass turbofans
Performance: maximum cruising speed 720km/h (447mph); maximum operating altitude 11,000m (36,100ft); take-off distance at maximum weight 1,200m (4,000ft); range with maximum payload 1,000km (620 miles); range with maximum fuel 3,200km (1,990 miles)
Weights: maximum take-off 30,500kg (67,240lb); take-off weight for 1,000m (3,280ft) runway, 26,500kg (58,420lb); maximum payload 7,500kg (16,534lb)
Dimensions: span 25.83m (84ft 9in); length 26.58m (87ft 2.5in); height 8.24m (27ft)
History: a specialised cargo transport, the An-72 is the bureau's first jet-powered transport with the two engines located forward and above the wing; which, combined with the trailing edge flaps, produces increased lift and enables the aircraft to operate off short runways. The double main wheels are on separate legs, enabling greater use of unprepared runways. The An-74 variant with a revised wing and longer fuselage has been developed for Arctic use.

The An-72 'Coaler' with engines sited high on the wings

Antonov An-124 'Condor'

Country of origin: USSR
Entered service: December 1982
Production: number of aircraft delivered, 20; in service, 15
Powerplant: four 23,430kgp (51,650lb st) Lotarev D-18T turbofans
Performance: cruise speed 850km/h (459kt) at 12,000m (39,370ft); range 4,500km (2,428 naut miles) with maximum payload
Weights: maximum take-off 450,000kg (892,863lb); payload up to 150,000kg (330,686lb)
Dimensions: span 73.3m (240.49ft); length 69.5m (228.02ft); wing area 628m² (6,760sq ft)
Seating capacity: 88 in upper cabin
History: the world's largest aircraft when introduced at the end of 1982, it was designed to take over from the An-22, which it resembles although it sports four large turbofans in place of the four turboprops. Despite its size, the An-124 is built with multi-wheeled landing gear, to effect operation from poor airstrips.

An Antonov An-124 Condor, a stopgap between the An-22 and the An-225

Antonov An-225 Mriya

Country of origin: USSR
First flight: December 1988
Powerplant: six 24,400kgp (53,800lb st)
Lotarev D-18 turbofans
Performance: cruising speed 700km/h
(378kt); range 4,500km (2,428 miles) with
200,000kg (440,920lb) payload
Weights: maximum take-off 600,000kg
(1,322,772lb); payload up to 250,000kg
(551,145lb)
Dimensions: span 84.4m (290ft); length 84m
(275.6ft)
History: now the world's largest aeroplane,
succeeding the An-124 'Condor', it utilises the
same engines as the An-124 but has an additional pair, and the new fuselage sports twin fins
on a large vertical endplate which enables loads
to be carried outside, on top of the fuselage.
Despite its size, the An-225 is able to utilise poor
airstrips, owing to a multi-wheel undercarriage.

*The huge Mriya, capable of
operating from a 1,000m (3,285ft)*
runway

BAC (Vickers) VC10

Country of origin: UK
First flight: June 1962
Entered service: April 1964 with BOAC
Powerplant: four 9,888kgp (21,800lb) RCo43D Mk 550 turbofans
Performance: high-speed cruise 935km/h (581mph) at 9,450m (31,000ft); long-range cruise 886km/h (550mph) at 11,600m (38,000ft); range with maximum payload 7,600km (4,720 miles); range with maximum fuel 11,470km (7,128 miles)
Weights: operating empty 71,940kg (158,594lb); maximum take-off 151,950kg (335,000lb); maximum payload 27,360kg (60,321lb); maximum landing 107,500kg (237,000lb)
Dimensions: span 44.55m (146ft 2in); length 52.32m (171ft 8in); height 12.04m (39ft 6in); wing area 272.4m² (2,932 sq ft)
Seating capacity: up to 187
History: the VC10 was the world's first rear-engined long-range intercontinental jet transport, making its inaugural flight on the London-Lagos route. The Super VC10 first flew on 7 May 1964 and entered service with BOAC on 1 April 1965. The Super VC10 was 3.96m (13ft) longer and could carry an additional 35 passengers.

The Super VC10s were only supplied to BOAC (17) and East African Airways (five)

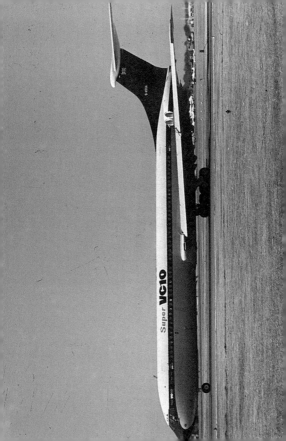

Boeing 707-320C

Country of origin: USA
First flight: July 1954
Production: 725 built; 270 in service
Powerplant: four 8,165kgp (18,000lb st) Pratt & Whitney JT3D-3 or 8,618kgp (19,000lb st) JT3D-7 turbofans
Performance: maximum cruising speed 965km/h (600mph); best economy cruise 886km/h (550mph); initial rate of climb 20.3m/sec (4,000ft/min); service ceiling 11,885m (39,000ft); range with maximum payload 6,920km (4,300 miles)
Weights: basic operating 62,872-66,224kg (136,610-146,000lb); maximum payload (passenger) 38,100kg (84,000lb) and (cargo) 41,453kg (91,390lb); maximum take-off 151,315kg (333,600lb)
Dimensions: span 44.42m (145ft 8.5in); length 45.6m (152ft 11in); height 12.94m (42ft 5.5in); wing area 283.4m² (3,050sq ft)
Seating capacity: up to 189 in one class
History: the Boeing 707 is regarded as the world's first effective long-range jet transport; although beaten into service by the de Havilland Comet, it is the 707 that is held responsible for the biggest breakthrough in passenger travel. Major variants include the 707-320C, a convertible or freighter variant with turbofans.

The Boeing 707, which entered service with Pan American

Boeing 727-200

Country of origin: USA
First flight: February 1963
Production: number built, 1,831; on order, nil
Powerplant: three 6,804kgp (15,000lb st) Pratt & Whitney JT8D-11 or 7,030kgp (15,500lb st) JT8D-15 or 7,257kgp (16,000lb st) JT8D-17 turbofans
Performance: maximum cruising speed 964km/h (599mph) at 7,530m (24,700ft); economy cruise 917km/h (570mph) at 9,145m (30,000ft); initial rate of climb 13.2m/sec (2,600ft/min); service ceiling 10,210m (33,500ft); range with maximum payload over 4,500km (2,800 miles)
Weights: operating empty 45,360kg (100,000lb); maximum payload 19,414kg (42,800lb); maximum take-off 95,027kg (209,500lb)
Dimensions: span 32.92m (108ft); length 46.69m (153ft 2in); height 10.36m (34ft); wing area 157.9m² (1,700sq ft)
Seating capacity: 125
History: a partner to the Model 707, it uses the same fuselage section but has three rear-mounted engines, a T-tail and a clean wing with triple- slotted trailing-edge flaps. The Model 727-200 was 6.1m (20ft) longer than the Model 727-100, and first entered service with Northern on 14 December 1967.

Boeing 737-200

Country of origin: USA
First flight: April 1967
Production: number delivered, 1,726; on order, 501
Powerplant: two 6,350kgp (14,000lb st) Pratt & Whitney JT8D-7 or 6,577kgp (14,400lb st) JT8D-9 or 7,030kgp (15,500lb st) JT8D-15 turbofans
Performance: maximum cruising speed 927km/h (576mph) at 6,890m (22,600ft); best economy cruise 890km/h (553mph); initial rate of climb 19.1m/sec (3,760ft/min); range with maximum payload 3,851km (2,370 miles); range with maximum fuel 4,705km (2,530 miles)
Dimensions: span 28.35m (93ft); length 30.48m (100ft); height 11.28m (37ft); wing area 91.05m² (980sq ft)
Seating capacity: 119
History: the world's best-selling airliner, with orders of nearly 2,500 in five variants. Intended for short-haul sectors, the Model 737 is distinguished by a fuselage section similar to that of the 707 and 727 Models, with turbofan pods mounted onto the under surfaces of the wings. The 737-200 entered service with United on 28 April 1969.

The Model 737 shares about 60 per cent commonality with the 727

Boeing 747-200

Country of origin: USA
First flight: February 1969
Production: 805 delivered; 299 on order
Powerplant: four from the range of 19,730kgp (43,500lb st) Pratt & Whitney JT9D-3 to 21,620kgp (47,670lb st) JT9D-7A turbofans
Performance: maximum speed 978km/h (608mph) at 9,145m (30,000ft); best economy cruise 935km/h (580mph); cruise ceiling 13,705m (45,000ft); range with maximum payload 8,023km (4,985 miles)
Weights: maximum payload 71,940kg (158,600lb); maximum take-off 356,070kg (785,000lb)
Dimensions: span 59.64m (195ft 8in); length 70.51m (231ft 4in); height 19.33m (63ft 5in); wing area 511m² (5,500sq ft)
Seating capacity: 350+
History: affectionately known as the 'Jumbo', the 747 is the world's largest airliner, bearing the brunt of the western world's long-range, high-capacity routes. It introduced the wide-body concept. The 747-200 version first entered service with KLM in 1971. The latest variant, the 747-400, has a two-crew flight deck with the latest electronic displays and instrumentation, extended wings and lean-burn turbofans.

Initially designed as a 430-seat type, accommodation varies considerably

Boeing 757

Country of origin: USA
First flight: February 1982
Production: number delivered, 312; on order, 360
Powerplant: two Rolls-Royce RB 211-535C turbofans, each rated at 16,980kgp (37,400lb st)
Performance: cruising speed 899km/h (540mph) at 10,670m (35,000ft); range with maximum payload about 2,000km (1,250 miles)
Weights: typical operating weight empty 61,290kg (135,000lb); maximum take-off 99,880kg (220,000lb); maximum zero-fuel 83,536kg (184,000lb); maximum landing weight 89,892kg (198,000lb)
Dimensions: span 37.95m (124ft 6in); overall length 47.32m (155ft 3in); overall height 13.56m (44ft 6in); wing area 181.25m² (1,951sq ft)
Seating capacity: 186
History: a narrow-body type with the same fuselage diameter as Models 707, 727 and 737, it was initially offered in both long and short-fuselage variants, with the latter being dropped owing to lack of customers. The fuel-efficient 757 entered service in December 1982.

The 757 is offered in versions with three maximum weights, fuel loads
and ranges

Boeing 767

Country of origin: USA
First flight: September 1981
Production: 375 delivered; 268 on order
Powerplant: two Pratt & Whitney JT9D-7R4A turbofans, each rated at 20,112kgp (44,300lb st) for take-off
Performance: cruising speed Mach 0.8 at 11,887m (39,000ft); design range 3,700km (2,300 miles)
Weights: operating empty 78,397kg (172,680lb); maximum payload 27,694kg (61,000lb); maximum take-off 128,030kg (282,000lb); maximum zero-fuel 109,870kg (242,000lb); maximum landing weight 116,680kg (257,000lb)
Dimensions: span 47.24m (155ft); length 48.46m (159ft); overall height 15.38m (50ft 5in)
Seating capacity: 200
History: a wide-body type planned in unison with the 757 for maximum commonality – pilots can obtain a single rating for both types. As with the 757, a shorter-fuselage variant was planned but dropped. The 767-300 provides greater seating capacity with a fuselage stretched by 6.42m (21ft 1in). The 767 entered service with United Airlines in August 1982.

The 767 was Boeing's first of the new generation of advanced technology airliners

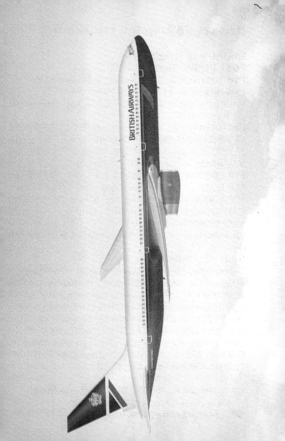

British Aerospace HS 125 Srs 700

Country of origin: UK
First flight: August 1962
Production: number ordered, 623 all versions
Powerplant: two Garrett-AiResearch TFE731-3-1H turbofans, each rated at 1,680kgp (3,700lb st) for take-off
Performance: maximum speed 592km/h (368mph) at sea level; service ceiling 12,500m (41,000ft); range with maximum payload 3,556km (2,210 miles)
Weights: empty operating 5,747kg (12,670lb); maximum payload 1,068kg (2,335lb); maximum take-off 10,977kg (24,200lb); maximum landing 9,979kg (22,000lb)
Dimensions: span 14.33m (47ft); length 15.46m (50ft 8.5in); wing area 32.8m² (353sq ft)
Seating capacity: 8
History: the most successful post-World War II civil aircraft of British origin, it began with de Havilland as a long-range executive transport. The first DH125 production craft were designated Srs10 and were powered by Viper 520 engines. The prototype Srs 700 first flew on 28 June 1976 powered by TFE 731 engines. The Srs 800 followed, powered by TFE 731-5 turbofans, the fuselage slightly lengthened and the wingspan increased by 1.32m (4ft 4in) and the gross weight increased by 909kg (2,000lb).

British Aerospace Trident 2E

Country of origin: UK
First flight: January 1967
Production: number built, 117; in airline service, 27
Powerplant: three 5,425kg (11,960lb) thrust Rolls-Royce RB163-25 Mk 512-5W Spey turbofans
Performance: cruising speed 974km/h (605mph) at 7,620m (25,000ft); economic cruising speed 959km/h (596mph) at 9,145m (30,000ft); range with typical payload and fuel reserves 3,965km (2,464 miles)
Weights: empty operating 33,203kg (73,200lb); maximum take-off 65,317kg (144,000lb)
Dimensions: span 29.87m (98ft); length 34.98m (114ft 9in); height 8.23m (27ft); wing area 135.26m² (1,456sq ft)
Seating capacity: 139
History: scaled down to fulfil BEA requirements, the Trident was not the commercial success that the original concept might have been. Highly distinctive, the aircraft had a T-tail and three turbofans grouped in the tail to leave the wings clean, as high-performance lifting surfaces fitted with advanced high-lift devices. The 2E entered service with BEA on 18 April 1968.

The Trident, built specifically to
BEA's requirements

British Aerospace One-Eleven 500

Country of origin: UK
First flight: August 1963
Production: number built, 230; in airline service, 123
Powerplant: two 5,693kg (12,550lb) thrust Rolls-Royce Spey Mk 512 DW turbofans
Performance: maximum cruising speed 871km/h (541mph) at 6,400m (21,000ft); maximum cruising height 10,670m (35,000ft); range with fuel reserves and full payload 2,726km (1,694 miles)
Weights: empty operating 24,386kg (53,762lb) maximum take-off 47,400kg (104,500lb)
Dimensions: span 28.5m (93ft 6in); length 32.61m (107ft); height 7.47m (24ft 6in); wing area 95.78m² (1,031sq ft)
Seating capacity: 119
History: originally designed by Hunting Aircraft Ltd as a four-abreast 48-seat airliner, with a 1,610-km (1,000-mile) range, the One-Eleven series 200 aircraft entered service on 9 April 1965. Variants include the Series 300, first ordered by American Airlines and altered to meet US regulations, and the Series 500 which appeared in 1966 with a stretched fuselage, increased by 4.11m (13ft 6in), and wingspan increased by 1.2m (5ft).

The BAC One-Eleven pioneered the
aft engine/T-tail combination

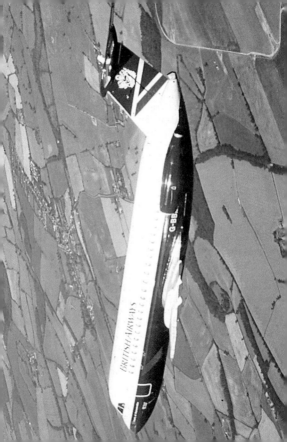

British Aerospace BAe 146 Srs 100

Country of origin: UK
First flight: September 1981
Production: number delivered, 142; on order, 41
Powerplant: four Avro Lycoming ALF502R-3 turbofans rated at 3,040kgp (6,700lb st) for take-off; fuel capacity 11,450 litres (2,540 Imp gal)
Performance: maximum operating speed Mach 0.7; economic cruising speed 708km/h (440mph) at 9,145m (30,000ft); range with fuel reserves and maximum payload 797km (495 miles)
Weights: empty operating 21,319kg (47,000lb); maximum take-off 37,308kg (82,250lb)
Dimensions: span 36.34m (118ft 1.3in); length 26.16m (85ft 10in); height 8.61m (28ft 3in); wing area 77.29m² (832sq ft)
Seating capacity: 93
History: four highly-efficient and quiet turbofans power BAe's short-range airliner, first developed by Hawker Siddeley. Now successfully established in three variants, the 146-100, 146-200 and 146-300, each successive variant has had the fuselage further lengthened to carry extra passengers.

The British Aerospace BAe 146 'whisperjet', on display at the 1988 Farnborough Air Show

Canadair 601 Challenger

Country of origin: Canada
First flight: November 1978
Powerplant: two Avro Lycoming ALF 502L turbofans, each rated at 3,405kgp (7,500lb st)
Performance: maximum cruising speed 488km/h (561mph) above 10,900m (36,000ft); maximum ratified ceiling 14,935m (47,000ft); maximum range 6,667km (4,143 miles)
Weights: operating empty 9,172kg (20,220lb); maximum payload, with maximum fuel, 427kg (940lb); maximum take-off 16,329kg (36,000ft); maximum landing 14,970kg (33,000lb)
Dimensions: span 18.84m (61ft 10in); length 20.85m (68ft 5in); height 6.3m (20ft 8in); wing area 41.81m² (450sq ft)
Seating capacity: 28
History: originally designated the LearStar 600, and designed by Bill Lear, the production and marketing rights were sold to Canadair Ltd in 1976. The only major design alteration was to switch to a T-tail. The 'bizjet' offers long range and comfort with a capacious cabin and good headroom. The CL-601 has drag-reducing winglets and is powered by 3,924kg (8,650lb) thrust General Electric CF34-1A turbofans.

The Canadair 601-3A was offered in a number of roles including air ambulance, maritime surveillance
and airborne early warning

Cessna Citation I

Country of origin: USA
First flight: September 1969
Powerplant: two Pratt & Whitney (Canada) JT15D-1A turbofans, each rated at 998kgp (2,200lb st) for take-off
Performance: maximum cruising speed 650km/h (404mph); initial rate of climb 13.6m/sec (2,680ft/min); maximum operating altitude 12,505m (41,000ft); maximum range 2,470km (1,535 miles)
Weights: empty operating 2,935kg (6,464lb); maximum take-off 5,834kg (12,850lb); maximum landing 5,153kg (11,350lb)
Dimensions: span 14.36m (47ft 1in); length 13.27m (43ft 6in); height 4.37m (14ft 2.4in)
Seating capacity: 8
History: launched as the Fanjet 500 by Cessna in October 1968 as a purely business jet, deliveries commenced in September 1971. The model 501 Citation 1 incorporated uprated engines and a wingspan increased by 2.21m (7ft 3in); it entered service in 1977. The Cessna Citation II, with stretched fuselage and uprated engines, was introduced in February 1978 with a seating capacity of 10. It had increased wingspan and 1,134kg (2,500lb) thrust JT51-D-4 engines. The Citation III of 1982 was revised with 1,656kg (3,650lb) thrust Garrett TFE731-3B-100S turbofans.

Dassault-Breguet Falcon 20

Country of origin: France
First flight: May 1963
Production: 500+
Powerplant: two General Electric CF700-2D-2 turbofans, each rated at 1,960kgp (4,315lb st) for take-off
Performance: maximum cruising speed 862km/h (536mph) at 7,620m (25,000ft); maximum range 3,570km (2,230 miles)
Weights: empty operating 7,240kg (15,970lb); maximum payload 1,500kg (3,320lb); maximum take-off 13,000kg (28,660lb)
Dimensions: span 16.3m (53ft 6in); length 17.15m (56ft 3in); height 5.32m (17.5in); wing area 41m² (440sq ft)
Seating capacity: 12
History: Dassault-Breguet's first business jet, the Falcon 20 or Mystère XX, as it is known in France, entered service in June 1965. The aircraft has proved to be very successful, with many variants being produced, prior to the introduction of the scaled-down Falcon 10 aircraft, which entered service in 1973.

A Falcon in use by the French
52 *Coastguard*

Dassault-Breguet Mercure 100

Country of origin: France
First flight: May 1971
Production: number built, 11; in airline service, 11
Powerplant: two 7,030kgp (15,500llb st) Pratt & Whitney JT8D-15 turbofans
Performance: maximum cruising speed 932km/h (579mph) at 6,096m (20,000ft); best economy cruise 858km/h (533mph) at 9,145m (30,000ft); initial rate of climb 16.76m/sec (3,300ft/min) at 45,359kg (100,000lb) weight; range with maximum payload 750km (466 miles); range with maximum fuel 1,650km (1,025 miles)
Weights: basic operating 31,800kg (70,107lb); maximum payload 16,200kg (35,715lb); maximum take-off 56,500kg (124,560lb)
Dimensions: span 30.55m (100ft 3in); length 34.84m (114ft 3.5in); height 11.36m (37ft 3.25in); wing area 116m² (1,249sq ft)
Seating capacity: 155
History: production aircraft entered service with Air Inter on 4 June 1974 with JT8D-15 turbofans; development had been financed largely by the French government and European Airlines. The internal French airline, Air Inter, remains the only operator.

One of the few Dassault-Breguet Mercure 100s

de Havilland D.H.106 Comet 4

Country of origin: UK
First flight: July 1949
Powerplant: four 4,649kgp (10,250lb st) Rolls-Royce Avon RA29 turbojets
Performance: cruising speed 809km/h (503mph) at 12,802m (42,000ft); service ceiling 13,411m (44,000ft); range 5,190km (3,225 miles) with full load of up to 9,206kg (20,286lb)
Weights: empty 34,200kg (75,400lb); maximum take-off 72,575kg (160,000lb)
Dimensions: span 35m (114.83ft); length 33.99m (111.5ft); wing area 197m² (2,121sq ft)
Seating capacity: 78 passengers
History: the Comet was the world's first turbojet-powered airliner. The type first flew with de Havilland Ghost turbojets and entered service as the Comet 1 with a seating capacity of 48. Three crashes during 1953/4 grounded the aircraft but a stretched 70-seat version, Comet 2, appeared after the fault was diagnosed and corrected, and the Comet 4 transatlantic version entered service in May 1958.

The Intercontinental Comet 4 of BOAC made its inaugural transatlantic flight on 14 November 1958, with services to the Far East 56 *commencing on 1 April 1959*

Douglas DC-8 Srs 50

Country of origin: USA
First flight: May 1958
Production: number built, 556 (all DC-8 versions); in airline service, 205
Powerplant: four 7,945kgp (17,000lb st) Pratt & Whitney JT3D-1 or 8,172kgp (18,000lb st) JT3D-3 or 3B turbofans
Performance: maximum cruising speed 933km/h (580mph); range with maximum payload 9,950km (6,185 miles)
Weights: maximum weight limited payload 21,092kg (46,500lb); maximum take-off 147,415kg (325,000lb)
Dimensions: span 43.41m (142ft 5in); length 45.87m (150ft 6in); height 12.91m (42ft 4in); wing area 266.5m² (2,868sq ft)
Seating capacity: 117
History: first ordered by Pan American on 13 October 1955, other airlines quickly followed, including KLM, SAS and JAL. The original DC-8 Srs 10 was powered by four Pratt & Whitney J57 turbojet engines, and the DC-8 entered service with both United and Delta on 18 September 1959. The Srs 50, with JT3D turbofans, which gave greatly improved thrust and fuel economy, was introduced together with a passenger/freight Srs 50 called the Jet Trader, which first flew on 29 October 1962.

*Right **a Douglas DC-8 model of pre-***
58 *   **McDonnell years***

Fokker F.28 Fellowship Mk 1000

Country of origin: Netherlands
First flight: May 1967
Production: 241 built; 191 in service
Powerplant: two 4,468kgp (9,850lb st) Rolls-Royce Spey 555-15 turbofans
Performance: maximum cruising speed 849km/h (528mph) at 6,400m (21,000ft); best economy cruise 836km/h (519mph) at 7,620m (25,000ft); long-range cruise 676km/h (420mph) at 9,145m (30,000ft); maximum service ceiling 10,670m (35,000ft); range with maximum payload 1,538km (956 miles); range with maximum fuel 1,945km (1,208 miles)
Weights: maximum payload 8,936kg (19,700lb); maximum take-off 29,480kg (65,000lb)
Dimensions: span 23.58m (77ft 4.25in); length 21.9m (89ft 10.75in); height 8.47m (27ft 9.5in); wing area 76.4m² (822sq ft)
Seating capacity: 60
History: the Fellowship entered service with LTU of Germany in February 1969 as a short-haul airliner with five-abreast, one-class seating. The stretched-fuselage version Mk 2000 entered service with Nigeria Airways in October 1972, and the Mk 4000 entered service with Linjeflyg of Sweden at the end of 1976.

The F.28 Fellowship was replaced by the highly upgraded F.100, announced in 1983

Fokker F.100

Country of origin: Netherlands
First flight: November 1986
Production: number of aircraft delivered, 51; on order, 155
Powerplant: two 6,282kgp (13,850lb st) Rolls-Royce Tay 620-15 turbofans
Performance: maximum cruising speed 800km/h (432kt) at 10,670m (35,000ft); range with maximum payload 2,015km (1,099 naut miles); range with maximum fuel 3,745km (2,022 naut miles)
Weights: operating empty 23,250kg (51,260lb); maximum take-off 41,500kg (91,500lb); maximum landing 38,330kg (84,500lb)
Dimensions: span 28.08m (92ft 1.5in); length 35.53m (116ft 6.5in); height 8.5m (27ft 10.5in); wing area 94.3m² (1,014.7sq ft)
Seating capacity: 107
History: the F.100 entered service with Swissair and featured single-class seating, five abreast. This updated F.28 features digital electronics, a four-screen electronic flight instrument system and an autoflight system that provides Cat II operation with Cat III update with autothrottle fitting.

Although Swissair was the first airline to take delivery of the F.100, US Air and American were the first big purchasers in North America

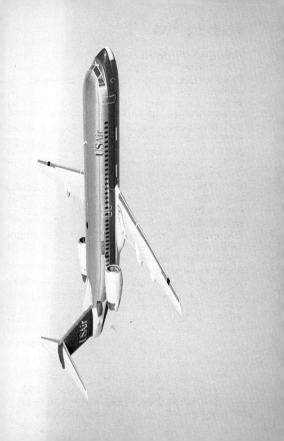

Gates Learjet 24F

Country of origin: USA
First flight: October 1963
Powerplant: two General Electric CJ610-6 turbojets, each rated at 1,340kgp (2,950lb st) for take-off
Performance: maximum operating speed 877km/h (545mph) at 9,450m (31,000ft); initial rate of climb 34.5m/sec (6,800ft/min); service ceiling 8,230m (27,000ft); range with maximum payload 2,728km (1,695 miles)
Weights: empty operating 3,234kg (7,130lb); maximum payload 1,755kg (3,870lb); maximum take-off 6,123kg (13,500lb); maximum landing weight 5,388kg (11,880lb)
Dimensions: span 10.84m (35ft 7in); length 13.18m (43ft 3in); height 3.73m (12ft 3in); wing area 21.53m² (231.8sq ft)
Seating capacity: 6
History: designed in Switzerland by William P Lear as one of the smallest and fastest business jets, the first deliveries were made in 1964. Just over 100 were manufactured before the Model 24 was introduced with uprated engines and a two-pilot crew. The stretched fuselage version, the Model 25, first flew in August 1966 with seating capacity for 8 passengers. The 20 series Learjets became the best-selling business jets.

Efficient, easy to maintain and easy to fly

Gates Learjet 55C Longhorn

Country of origin: USA
First flight: April 1979
Powerplant: two 1,678kgp (3,700st lb) Garrett-AiResearch TFE 731-3A-2B turbofans
Performance: cruising speed 885km/h (550mph); maximum ceiling 15,550m (51,000ft); initial rate of climb 25.5m/sec (5,020ft/min); range 4,170km (2,250 naut miles) with 1,079kg (2,378lb) payload
Weights: empty 5,725kg (12,662lb); maximum take-off 9,526kg (21,000lb)
Dimensions: span 13.34m (43ft 9.5in); length 16.79m (55ft 1.5in); height 4.47m (14ft 8in); wing area 24.57m² (264.5sq ft)
Seating capacity: 10
History: designed with stand-up headroom, unlike the Series 20 and 30 models, the Learjet 55 provides a higher standard of comfort. Put in hand in 1977, it has a cabin length of 4.93m (16ft 2.5in). One drawback of the 55C Longhorn is the 1,708m (5,600ft) of field runway required for take-off compared to the 1,213m (3,977ft) required by the Model 25D.

The bigger, upgraded and most comfortable of the Learjet family

Grumman Gulfstream II

Country of origin: USA
First flight: October 1966
Powerplant: two Rolls-Royce Spey Mk 511-8 turbofans, each rated at 5,175kgp (11,400lb st) for take-off
Performance: maximum cruising speed 936km/h (581mph) at 7,620m (25,000ft); initial rate of climb 22.1m/sec (4,350ft/min); service ceiling 13,100m (43,000ft); range with maximum fuel 6,880km (4,275 miles)
Weights: maximum take-off 29,711kg (65,500lb); maximum landing 26,535kg (58,500lb)
Dimensions: span 20.98m (68ft 10in); length 24.36m (79ft 11in); height 7.47m (24ft 6in); wing area 75.21m² (809.6sq ft)
Seating capacity: 10
History: launched in May 1965 to succeed the Gulfstream I, the Gulfstream II was of similar dimensions but with seating capacity for up to 19 in high-density layout. It entered service in December 1966. In 1978, optional tip tanks were made available, adding almost 1,000km (621 miles) to the range. More than 250 Gulfstream IIs were built, many of them refitted as II-B with the advanced wing of the III. The III first flew in December 1979 with seating for 19. Further development gave the Gulfstream IV, with Rolls-Royce Tay Mk 611-8 turbofans.

Ilyushin Il-62 Classic

Country of origin: USSR
First flight: January 1963
Production: 228+ built; 17 in service
Powerplant: four 10,500kgp (23,150lb st) Kuznetsov NK-8-4 turbofans
Performance: typical cruising speed 850-900km/h (528-560mph) at 10,000-12,000m (33,000-39,400ft); range with maximum payload, and one-hour fuel reserve, 6,700km (4,160 miles); range with maximum fuel 9,200km (5,715 miles)
Weights: maximum payload 23,000kg (50,700lb); maximum take-off 162,000kg (357,000lb); maximum landing 105,000kg (232,000lb)
Dimensions: span 43.2m (141ft 9in); length 53.12m (174ft 3.5in); height 12.35m (40ft 6.25in); wing area 279.6m² (3,010sq ft)
Seating capacity: 168
History: the Il-62 was the first long-range four-engined jet developed by the Soviet Union for commercial use. The contemporary of the Boeing 707, the DC-10 and the VC10, it entered service with Aeroflot on 15 September 1967. First used on the Moscow-Montreal route, the Il-62 replaced the Tu-114s on the Moscow-New York route in 1968.

The Il-62MK of 1978 introduced considerable modifications to permit operations at higher weights

Ilyushin Il-76T 'Candid'

Country of origin: USSR
First flight: March 1971
Production: number built, 600; in airline service, 250
Powerplant: four Soloviev D-30KP turbofans, each rated at 12,000kgp (26,455lb st) for take-off
Performance: typical cruising speed 850km/h (528mph) at 13,000m (42,650ft); take-off run, unpaved runway, 850m (2,790ft); landing run, unpaved runway, 450m (1,476ft); typical range with maximum payload 5,000km (3,100 miles)
Weights: maximum payload 40,000kg (88,185lb); maximum take-off 157,000kg (346,125lb)
Dimensions: span 50.5m (165ft 8in); length 46.59m (152ft 10.5in); height 14.76m (48ft 5in); wing area 300m² (3,229.2sq ft)
History: this is primarily a specialised freighter used by the Soviet Air Force (Il-76M variant). It is expected to perform tanker duties for flight refuelling and also to be the basis for an airborne warning and control system. Some 20 variants are thought to have been produced, and the aircraft is currently in service with four Middle East airlines, in addition to Aeroflot and Cubana.

Variants include the 'Mainstay' early warning system and Il-78 inflight refuelling tanker

Ilyushin Il-86 'Camber'

Country of origin: USSR
First flight: December 1976
Production: number estimated to have been built 65; on order, 35
Powerplant: four Kuznetsov NK-86 turbofans, each rated at 13,000kgp (28,635lb st) for take-off
Performance: cruising speed 900-950km/h (560-590mph) at 9,145m (30,000ft); range 3,600km (2,235 miles) with full passenger payload
Weights: maximum payload 42,000kg (92,500lb); gross weight 206,000kg (454,145lb)
Dimensions: span 48.06m (157ft 8.25in); length 59.54m (195ft 4in); height 15.81m (51ft 10.5in); wing area 320m² (3,444sq ft)
Seating capacity: 350
History: the first, and only, Soviet wide-body commercial aircraft, it entered service with Aeroflot in December 1980, operating between Moscow and Tashkent. The first international service between Moscow and East Berlin was flown on 3 July 1981.

The Il-86-300 long-range variant is now designated Il-96

Lockheed L-1011-1 Tristar

Country of origin: USA
First flight: November 1970
Production: 250 built; 237 in service
Powerplant: three 19,050kgp (42,000lb st) Rolls-Royce RB211-22B or 19,730kgp (43,500lb st) RB211-22F turbofans
Performance: maximum cruising speed 925km/h (575mph) at 10,670m (35,000ft); range with maximum payload 4,629km (2,878 miles); range with maximum fuel 7,189km (4,467 miles) 18,145kg (40,000lb) payload
Weights: operating empty 106,265kg (234,275lb); maximum payload 41,150kg (90,725lb); maximum take-off 195,045kg (430,000lb)
Dimensions: span 47.34m (155ft 4in); length 54.35m (178ft 8in); height16.87m (55ft 4in); wing area 320m² (3,456sq ft)
Seating capacity: 345
History: deliveries commenced on 5 April 1972 to Eastern, who inaugurated services with them on 26 April, two months ahead of TWA. The final two Tristars were delivered in June 1985. Development problems with the engines broke Rolls-Royce financially and nearly broke Lockheed, both companies having to be rescued by their respective governments.

*The final production model was the
L-1011-500 for very long-range
operations*

McDonnell Douglas DC-8 Super 70 Srs

Country of origin: USA
First flight: May 1982
Production: number converted, 110
Powerplant: four 10,886kg (24,000lb) thrust General Electric/SNECMA CFM56-2 turbofans
Performance: maximum speed 966km/h (600mph); cruising speed 855km/h (531mph) at 10,670m (35,000ft); range with maximum payload 11,619km (7,220 miles)
Weights: empty operating 69,218kg (152,600lb); maximum take-off 151,953kg (335,000lb)
Dimensions: span 45.24m (148ft 5in); length 47.98m (157ft 5in); height 12.93m (42ft 5in); wing area 271.92m² (2,927sq ft)
Seating capacity: 189
History: the DC-8 was produced in direct competition to the Boeing 707, but Douglas lacked the flexibility of Boeing and produced nine test aircraft and utilised three different types of aircraft before the primary variant, the DC-8-10 domestic model, was launched with Pratt & Whitney JT3C-6 turbojets. The stretched DC-8 Super 60 series of 1967 allowed conversion of Super 61, 62, and 63 aircraft with General Electric/SNECMA CFM56 turbofans, designated Super 71, 72 and 73.

The first McDonnell Douglas DC-8 Super 71 Srs to be refitted with CFM56 turbofans

78

McDonnell Douglas DC-9 Srs 50

Country of origin: USA
First flight: December 1974
Production: number built, 96; in airline service, 84
Powerplant: two 7,031kg (15,500lb) thrust Pratt & Whitney JT8D-15 turbofans
Performance: maximum speed 925km/h (575mph); economic cruising speed 821km/h (510mph); range with passengers and fuel reserves 3,323km (2,065 miles)
Weights: empty 28,068kg (61,880lb); maximum take-off 54,885kg (121,000lb)
Dimensions: span 28.47m (93ft 5in); length 40.72m (133ft 7.25in); height 8.53m (28ft); wing area 92.97m² (1,000.75sq ft)
Seating capacity: 139
History: the DC-9 Srs 10 powered by Pratt & Whitney JT8D-5 engines entered service with Delta on 8 December 1965. The Srs 30, with a fuselage stretched by 4.6m (14ft 11in) and with extended wing tips, first flew on 1 August 1967. The Srs 40, developed specifically for SAS, was 1.87m (6ft 4in) longer still; it first flew on 28 November 1967. The Srs 50, which was 1.87m (6ft 4in) longer than the Srs 40, entered service with Swissair on 24 August 1975.

Investment in the DC-9 forced the Douglas-McDonnell merger

McDonnell Douglas DC-9 Super 80 (MD-80)

Country of origin: USA
First flight: October 1979
Production: number delivered (all MD-80 series), 787; on order, 240
Powerplant: two 8,400kgp (18,500lb st) Pratt & Whitney JT8D-209 turbofans
Performance: maximum cruising speed 878km/h (546mph) at 9,450m (31,000ft); range with 137-passenger load, 3,306km (2,055 miles) at 10,670m (35,000ft)
Weights: maximum take-off 63,503kg (140,000lb); maximum landing weight 58,060kg (128,000lb); maximum zero-fuel weight 53,524kg (118,000lb)
Dimensions: span 32.85m (107ft 10in); length 45.08m (147ft 10in); height 8.93m (29ft 10in); wing area 118.8m² (1,279sq ft)
Seating capacity: 150
History: McDonnell Douglas continued development of the DC-9, and in 1977 entered production with the DC-9 Super 80, which entered service in 1980 with Swissair and was renamed the MD-80. Variants are the DC-9 Super 81 (now MD-81), with JT8D-209s and a 4.34m (14ft 3in) fuselage stretch; the DC-9 Super 82 (now MD-82), MD-83, MD-87 and MD-88.

Developments included an electronic flight instruments system, combined with flight-management computer and inertial navigation system

82

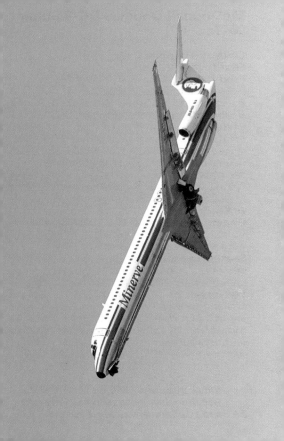

McDonnell Douglas DC-10 Srs 30

Country of origin: USA
First flight: August 1970
Production: 446 built; 412 in service
Powerplant: three 23,134kgp (51,000lb st) General Electric CF6-50C turbofans
Performance: maximum cruising speed 917km/h (570mph) at 9,450m (31,000ft); initial rate of climb 11.8m/sec (2,320ft/min); service ceiling 9,965m (32,700ft); range with maximum payload 6,875km (4,272 miles)
Weights: basic operating 119,334kg (263,087lb); maximum payload 47,587kg (104,913lb); maximum take-off 251,744kg (555,00lb)
Dimensions: span 40.42m (165ft 4in); length 55.35m (181ft 7in); height 17.7m (58ft 1in); wing area 364.3m² (3,921sq ft)
Seating capacity: 380
History: a transcontinental trijet developed to compete with Boeing's 747; the first orders were placed by American on 19 February 1968 and by United two months later. The DC-10 entered service with American Airlines on 5 August 1971, between Los Angeles and Chicago. The DC-10 Srs 30 was developed for European Airlines and has a wingspan increased by 3.08m (10ft) and a fractionally shorter fuselage.

Work began in 1966 on the DC-10 and has developed into the MD-11, with drag-reducing winglets for the 1990s

Rockwell Sabreliner 75A

Country of origin: USA
Powerplant: two General Electric CF700-2D-2 turbofans, each rated at 2,043kgp (4,500lb st) for take-off
Performance: maximum cruising speed 906km/h (563mph); initial rate of climb 22.9m/sec (4,500ft/min); maximum range 3,156km (1,960 miles)
Weights: operating empty 5,896kg (13,000lb); maximum take-off 10,580kg (23,300lb); maximum landing 9,988kg (22,000lb)
Dimensions: span 13.62m (44ft 8in); length 14.34m (47ft); height 5.26m (17ft 3in); wing area 31.78m² (342.05sq ft)
Seating capacity: 9
History: originally built to meet USAF requirements for a small trainer/transport, 200 aircraft were initially built for the USAF and USN. The stretched-fuselage Sabreliner 60 powered by JT12A-8 engines appeared in 1967, and the Sabreliner 70 in 1970, both designed to accommodate two additional passengers. The Sabreliner 70 was redesignated 75, and in 1973 the 75A, powered by the General Electric CF700-2D-2 turbofans.

The light but rugged, now ageing,
Sabreliner

Tupolev Tu-124

Country of origin: USSR
First flight: June 1960
Production: number produced, 180
Powerplant: two 5,400kg (11,905lb) Soloviev D-20P turbofans
Performance: maximum speed 907km/h (603mph); range with maximum payload 1,220km (760 miles); range with maximum fuel and 3,500kg (7,715lb) payload 2,100km (1,305 miles)
Weights: empty 22,500kg (49,600lb); maximum payload 6,000kg (13,228lb); maximum take-off 38,000kg (83,775lb); maximum landing 35,000kg (77,160lb)
Dimensions: span 25.55m (83ft 9.5in); length 30.58m (100ft 4in); height 8.08m (26ft 6in); wing area 119m² (1,281sq ft)
Seating capacity: 44
History: the Tu-124 entered service with Aeroflot on 2 October 1962 on the Moscow-Tallinn route, the first airliner in service powered by turbofan engines. A completely restructured design, the Tu-124 looked exactly like a smaller version of the Tu-104. The second production batch, designated Tu-124V, became the standard with an increased seating capacity of 56.

The Tu-124 on a visit to London's Heathrow airport was the forerunner of the Tu-134, which took over the 124's international duties

Tupolev Tu-144

Country of origin: USSR
First flight: December 1968
Production: number built, 13
Powerplant: four 20,000kgp (44,000lb st) Kuznetsov NK-44 turbofans with reheat
Performance: maximum cruising speed up to 2,500km/h (1,550mph) at altitudes of up to 18,000m (59,000ft); maximum range with full payload 6,500km (4,030 miles)
Weights: maximum take-off 180,000kg (396,830lb); maximum payload 14,000kg (30,865lb) maximum landing weight 120,000kg (264,550lb)
Dimensions: span 28.8m (94ft 6in); length 65.7m (215ft 6.5in); height 12.85m (42ft 2in); wing area 438m² (4,714.5sq ft)
Seating capacity: 140
History: the world's first supersonic airliner to fly, the SST Tu-144 resembles Concorde very closely, being only marginally larger and faster. The first production model was larger overall since its first prototype flight, with uprated relocated engines and new wings with straight leading edges. The Tu-144 entered service with Aeroflot on 26 December 1975 on the Moscow-Alma Ata route, but services were halted on 1 June 1978 immediately following an accident to one of the airliners.

The Tu-144 flights were never resumed following the crash

Tupolev Tu-154

Country of origin: USSR
First flight: October 1968
Production: 692 built; 672 in service
Powerplant: three 9,500kgp (20,950lb st) Kuznetsov NK-8-2 turbofans
Performance: range with maximum payload and one hour reserve 3,460km (2,150 miles); range with maximum fuel and 13,650kg (30,100lb) payload 5,280km (3,280 miles)
Weights: maximum payload 20,000kg (44,090lb); maximum fuel load 33,150kg (73,085lb); maximum take-off 90,000kg (198,416lb); maximum landing 80,000kg (176,370lb)
Dimensions: span 37.55m (123ft 2.5in); length 47.9m (157ft 1.75in); wing area 201.45m² (2,169sq ft)
Seating capacity: 128
History: entered full passenger service in February 1972, on the Moscow-Mineralnye Vady route, and international operation began on 1 August 1972 between Moscow and Prague. The Tu-154A entered service in 1975, having first flown in 1973, with uprated NK-8-2U engines, was followed in 1977 by the Tu-154B, with accommodation for up to 180 passengers in a single-class layout, and by the Tu-154M in 1982 with Soloviev D-30KU-154-11 engines.

A tri-jet airliner, the design for
92 *which goes back to 1964*

Aérospatiale Nord 262 Fregate

Country of origin: France
First flight: July 1960
Production: number built, 110; in airline service, 26
Powerplant: two 1,145ehp Turboméca Bastan VII turboprops
Performance: maximum speed 385km/h (239mph); cruising speed 375km/h (233mph); initial rate of climb 6.1m/sec (1,200ft/min); service ceiling 7,160m (23,500ft); range with maximum payload 975km (605 miles); range with maximum fuel 1,760km (1,095 miles)
Weights: basic operating weight 7,029kg (15,496lb); maximum payload 3,270kg (7,209lb); maximum take-off weight 10,600kg (23,370lb); maximum landing 10,300kg (22,710lb)
Dimensions: span (N262 A) 21.9m (71ft 10in); span (Fregate) 22.6m (74ft 1.75in); length 19.28m (63ft 3in); height 6.2m (20ft 4in); wing area (N262 A) 55m² (592sq ft); wing area (Fregate) 55.79m² (601sq ft)
Seating capacity: 24-26
History: developed by Nord Aviation out of the MH-260, it featured a pressurised circular-section fuselage. The Nord 262B entered service with Air Inter on 16 July 1964.

The Nord 262 Fregates were quickly replaced and many were purchased by developing airlines

Aérospatiale C-160 Transall

Country of origin: France/Germany
First flight: February 1963
Production: number ordered (civil version), 11; in airline service, 11
Powerplant: two Rolls-Royce Type RTY 20 Mk 22 turboprops, each rated at 6,200ehp for take-off
Performance: maximum speed 592km/h (367mph) at 4,875m (16,000ft); economical cruising speed 454km/h (282mph) at 6,096m (20,000ft); rate of climb 6.6m/sec (1,300ft/min); service ceiling 7,770m (25,500ft); range 4,800km (2,982 miles) with 8,000kg (17,637lb) payload, and 1,700km (1,056 miles) with 16,000kg (35,274lb)
Dimensions: span 40m (13ft 3in); length 32.4m (106ft 3.5in); height 12.36m (40ft 6.75in); wing area 160.1m² (1,723sq ft)
History: a joint development for both the German and the French military, with assembly lines set up in both countries. By 1970, about 170 aircraft had been produced, including nine for the South African Air Force. SOGERMA converted four of the C-160Fs of the Armée de l'Air for Air France, redesignated as C-160P, operating Paris-Bastia (Corsica) for mail-carrying 13.5 tons (1.8 million letters) nightly, loading and off-loading in about 12 minutes.

The Transall gets through a prodigious workload

Antonov An-24V

Country of origin: USSR
First flight: August 1960
Production: number built, 1,100+; in airline service, 850
Powerplant: two 2,500ehp Ivchenko A1-24 Seriiny II turboprops
Performance: maximum cruising speed 498km/h (310mph); best range cruise 450km/h (280mph) at 6,000m (19,700ft); initial climb rate 7.7m/sec (1,515ft/min); service ceiling 8,400m (27,560ft); range with maximum payload and reserves 550km (341 miles); range with maximum fuel and 45min reserve 2,400km (1,490 miles)
Weights: empty 13,300kg (29,320lb); maximum take-off 21,000kg (46,300lb)
Dimensions: span 29.2m (95ft 9.5in); length 23.53m (77ft 2.5in); height 8.32m (27ft 3.5in); wing area 74.98m² (807.1sq ft)
Seating capacity: 50
History: the An-24 entered service with Aeroflot in September 1963, and today Aeroflot has more An-24s than any other aircraft. Production continued until 1977, including the specialised freighter variants An-24T and An-24RT. The aircraft is still flown by 15 airlines.

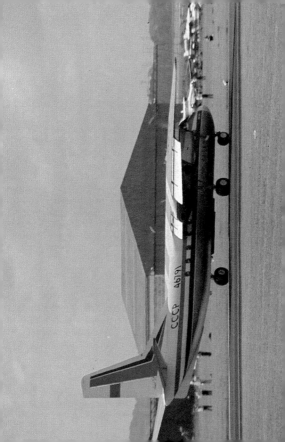

Avions de Transport Regional ATR 42-200

Country of origin: France/Italy
First flight: August 1984
Production: number delivered, 137; on order, 194
Powerplant: two 1,800shp PWAC PW 120 turboprops
Performance: maximum cruising speed 509km/h (316mph) at 6,096m (20,000ft); range with maximum payload 2,420km (1,500 miles); range with maximum fuel 5,566km (3,457 miles)
Weights: empty 9,609kg (21,184lb); ramp weight, 15,770kg (34,767lb); maximum take-off 15,570kg (34,723lb); maximum landing 15,500kg (34,175lb)
Dimensions: span 24.57m (80ft 6in); length 22.7m (74ft 5in); height 7.59m (24ft 9in); wing area 54.5m² (586sq st)
Seating capacity: 46
History: the ATR 42 entered service in 1986 in southern Europe and north America, after both French and Italian government-owned manufacturers had signed an agreement, in 1979, to develop a regional airliner. Aeritalia is responsible for the design and manufacture of the fuselage and the tail, with the final assembly being made in Toulouse.

Increasing in popularity, especially for feeder routes where the ATR 42 proves economical

Avions de Transport Regional ATR 72

Country of origin: France/Italy
First flight: 1985
Production: number ordered and on option, 21
Powerplant: two Pratt & Whitney (Canada) PW-124-2 turboprops
Performance: maximum cruising speed 530km/h (330mph); maximum range 2,778km (1,725 miles)
Weights: empty 12,200kg (26,931lb); maximum take-off 19,990-21,500kg (44,128-47,461lb)
Dimensions: span 27.05m (88ft 9in); length 27.16m (89ft 1in); height 7.65m (25ft 1in)
Seating capacity: 64-72
History: a stretched-fuselage version of the ATR 42: the first orders were placed by Finnair, and the ATR 72 took just three years from the decision by Aérospatiale and Aeritalia to proceed to first flight.

American Eagle was one of seven American companies to place early orders

BAC Vanguard Type 953

Country of origin: UK
First flight: May 1961
Production: number built, 44; 7 in service
Powerplant: four 5,545ehp Rolls-Royce Type 512 turboprops
Performance: range with maximum payload 2,945km (1,830 miles) at over 7,620m (25,000ft); range with maximum fuel 4,990km (3,100 miles) at 7,620m (25,000ft)
Weights: empty equipped 37,422kg (82,500lb); maximum payload 16,785kg (37,000lb); maximum take-off 66,448kg (146,500lb); maximum landing 61,238kg (130,500lb)
Dimensions: span 36.15m (118ft 7in); length 37.45m (122ft 10.5in); height 10.64m (34ft 11in); wing area 142m² (1,529sq ft)
Seating capacity: 120
History: delays owing to a defect in the Type 512 engine prevented the Type 951 from entering service with BEA until March 1961, although it had first flown on 20 January 1959. Already uncompetitive by the time it entered service, no further orders were obtained other than the initial launch order from BEA and an order from TLA, now Air Canada. Deliveries of the Vanguard 953 were completed in March 1962.

The Vanguard was never really successful, and will soon disappear from service altogether

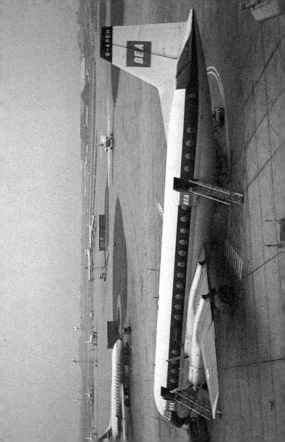

Beech King Air C90

Country of origin: USA
First flight: January 1964
Production: number built, 1,300+
Powerplant: two Pratt & Whitney (Canada) PT6A-12 turboprops, each rated at 550ehp for take-off
Performance: maximum cruising speed 412km/h (256mph) at 3,660m (12,000ft); initial rate of climb 9.9m/sec (1,955ft/min); service ceiling 8,565m (28,100ft); range with maximum fuel 1,773-2,227km (1,100-1,384 miles), depending on altitude; maximum range 2,374km (1,475 miles) at 6,400m (21,000ft)
Weights: empty 2,558kg (5,640lb); maximum take-off 4,377kg (9,650lb)
Dimensions: span 15.32m (50ft 3in); length 10.82m (35ft 6in); height 4.33m (14ft 2.5in); wing area 27.3m² (293.9sq ft)
Seating capacity: 6
History: a variant of the Beech Queen Air, but powered by PT6A-6 turboprop engines and with a pressurised cabin, designated Model 90. It was superseded by the A90 and B90, both powered by PT6A-20s. All variants were of similar dimensions and capable of seating 15 in high-density layout.

Right **is the Beech King Air Model A100, which had a reduced wingspan and a fuselage**
lengthened for 15 passengers

Beech Starship

Country of origin: USA

First flight: August 1983; FAA certificate granted 1989

Powerplant: two 1,100shp Pratt & Whitney (Canada) PT6A-67 turboprops

Performance: cruising speed 652km/h (405mph) at 7,620m (25,500ft); service ceiling 12,495m (41,000ft); range 2,089km (1,298 miles) with maximum payload of up to 1,264kg (2,884lb)

Weights: empty 4,044kg (8,916lb); maximum take-off 6,350kg (14,000lb)

Dimensions: span 16.46m (54ft); length 14.05m (46.08ft); wing area 25.09m² (280.9sq ft)

Seating capacity: 10

History: the impressive futuristic appearance of the Starship is a major departure from previous Beech aircraft, with swept canard and two pusher turboprops. The Starship's airframe comprises a high percentage of composite materials. Original test flights in 1983 were with an 85 per cent scale version developed by Burt Rutan's Scaled Composites Inc. The first flights with full-size pre-production aircraft took place in 1986.

The futuristic Starship, with its twin pusher turboprops

Beech Super King Air B200

Country of origin: USA
First flight: October 1972
Powerplant: two 850shp Pratt & Whitney (Canada) PT6A-42 turboprops
Performance: maximum cruise speed 536km/h (289ft) at 7,620m (25,000ft); range with maximum payload 1,418km (880 miles); range with maximum fuel 3,570km (2,217 miles)
Weights: empty operating 3,419kg (7,538lb); maximum take-off 5,670kg (12,500lb); maximum landing 5,670kg (12,500lb)
Dimensions: span 16.61m (54ft 7in); length 13.34m (43ft 9in); height 4.75m (15ft); wing area 28.15m² (303sq ft)
Seating capacity: 10
History: the King Air is used both as a business turboprop and as an airliner on low-density long-distance routes. The 200 has a greater wingspan than the 100, and was the first Beech craft to have a T-tail; it entered service in December 1973. A civil cargo version became available in 1979.

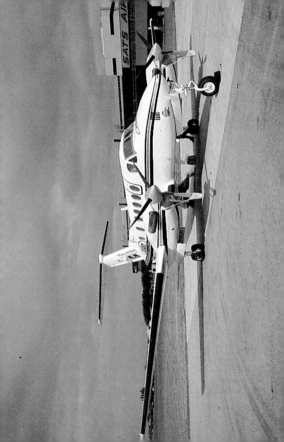

Bristol 175 Britannia Srs 310

Country of origin: UK
Production: number built, 100; in airline service, 9
Powerplant: four 4,450shp Bristol Proteus 765 turboprops
Performance: maximum cruising speed 639km/h (397mph); best economy cruise 575km/h (357mph); range with maximum payload 4,990km (3,100 miles); range with maximum fuel 5,327km (3,310 miles)
Weights: empty equipped 42,410kg (93,500lb); maximum payload 15,650kg (34,500lb); maximum take-off 83,915kg (185,000lb)
Dimensions: span 43.36m (142ft 3in); length 37.87m (124ft 3in); height 11.43m (37ft 6in); wing area 192.76m² (2,074sq ft)
Seating capacity: up to 139
History: the aircraft was first flown on 16 August 1952 as the Srs 100. The Srs 300 made its first flight on 31 December 1956. It had a stretched fuselage and uprated Proteus engines. BOAC was the largest purchaser of the 300, which was designated 310, the last two digits being the airline coding. The RAF also took delivery of 23 aircraft, which were subsequently sold off in 1975.

A Bristol Brittania Srs 100 of British Overseas Airways Company in the early 1950s

British Aerospace ATP

Country of origin: UK
First flight: August 1986
Production: number delivered, 25; on order, 14
Powerplant: two 2,520ehp Pratt & Whitney PW124/125 turboprops
Performance: maximum cruising speed 492km/h (266kt) at 4,672m (15,000ft); range with maximum payload 1,576km (851 naut miles); range with maximum fuel 4,386km (2,368 naut miles)
Weights: operating empty 13,595kg (29,970lb); ramp weight 22,589kg (49,800lb); maximum take-off 22,453kg (49,500lb); maximum landing 21,773kg (48,000lb)
Dimensions: span 30.63m (100ft 5in); length 26.01m (85ft 5in); height 7.14m (32ft 4in) wing area 71.3m² (843sq ft)
Seating capacity: 64
History: a stretched development of the BAe 748, the Advanced Turboprop received its go-ahead in March 1984. There is also a possibility that the ATP could be manufactured under licence in the USSR, where Aeroflot would use it to replace the ageing Il-14 and Il-24s.

Only purchased in small numbers, British Airways remains the biggest
operator

British Aerospace Jetstream 31

Country of origin: UK
First flight: August 1967
Production: number ordered 123
Powerplant: two 940shp Garrett TPE331 turboprops
Performance: maximum speed 210km/h (113kt); maximum cruising speed 486km/h (263kt) at 4,572m (15,000ft); range with maximum payload 1,519km (820 naut miles); range with maximum fuel 2,240km (1,391 miles)
Weights: empty operating 4,360kg (9,613lb); maximum take-off 6,950kg (15,322lb); maximum landing 6,600kg (14,500lb)
Dimensions: span 15.85m (52ft); length 14.36m (47ft 3in); wing area 25.2m² (271sq ft)
Seating capacity: 18
History: originally the Handley Page Jetstream, it entered service in 1969. Handley Page collapsed in 1970 after delivering only 38, with 10 more in production. In 1978 British Aerospace relaunched the Jetstream, with deliveries commencing in 1981. The latest development is the Jetstream 41, with a 4.87m (16ft) longer fuselage and seating for up to 29 passengers.

The success of the Jetstream is owed, to a large degree, to the
116 *Garrett engine*

British Aerospace 810 Viscount

Country of origin: UK
First flight: December 1957
Production: number built, 440; in airline service, 37
Powerplant: four 2,100ehp Rolls-Royce Dart 525 turboprops
Performance: cruising speed 563km/h (350mph) at 6,096m (20,000ft); maximum payload range 2,757km (1,725 miles); maximum fuel range 2,830km (1,760 miles)
Weights: basic operating 18,753kg (41,565lb); maximum take-off 32,886kg (72,500lb); maximum payload 6,577kg (14,500lb)
Dimensions: span 28.5m (93ft 8in); length 26.11m (85ft 8in); wing area 89.46m² (963sq ft)
Seating capacity: 65
History: the Vickers Viscount was the world's first turboprop transport, entering service with BEA on 18 April 1953 between London and Cyprus with a seating capacity of 47. The type 810 was the final variation, utilising more powerful engines.

The Type 810 version, with stretched fuselage, first flew in December 1957

British Aerospace BAe 748 Srs 2B

Country of origin: UK
First flight: June 1960
Production: number ordered, 381; in airline service, 162
Powerplant: two 1,700ekw (2,280eshp) Rolls-Royce Dart 536-2 turboprops
Performance: cruising speed at 17,237kg (38,000lb) weight, 452km/h (281mph); service ceiling 7,620m (25,000ft); range with maximum payload and fuel reserves 1,455km (904 miles)
Weights: empty operating 12,206kg (26,910lb); maximum take-off 21,092kg (46,500lb)
Dimensions: span 31.23m (102ft 5.5in); length 20.42m (67ft); height 7.57m (24ft 10in); wing area 77m² (828.87sq ft)
Seating capacity: 58
History: the first production model flew on 30 August 1961, and entered service with Skyways Coach-Air the following year. The Srs 2, with uprated engines, first flew as a converted Srs 1 on 6 November 1961, and entered service with BKS Air Transport the following year.

The 748 has been sold successfully throughout the world

Casa C-212-100 Aviocar

Country of origin: Spain
First flight: March 1971
Production: number built, 389
Powerplant: two 776ehp Garrett-AiResearch TPE331-5-251C turboprops
Performance: maximum speed 370km/h (230mph) at 3,660m (12,000ft); cruising speed 315km/h (196mph) at 3,660m (12,000ft); rate of climb 9.1m/sec (1,800ft/min); service ceiling 8,140m (26,000ft); range 480km (300 miles) with maximum payload
Weights: empty equipped 3,905kg (8,690lb); maximum payload 2,000kg (4,410lb) maximum take-off 6,500kg (14,330lb)
Dimensions: span 19m (62ft 4in); length 15.2m (49ft 10.5in); height 6.3m (20ft 8in); wing area 40m² (430.6sq ft)
Seating capacity: 19
History: the C-212-100 was initially put into production for the Spanish Air Force, and the first production model flew on 17 November 1972. Also built by Nurtanio in Indonesia, the C-212 is rugged and economical. Variants include the C-212A military transport, the C-212-100, the heavier C-212-10 (C-212-200), and the yet heavier C-212-300.

Casa-Nusantara Airtech CN-235

Country of origin: Spain/Indonesia
First flight: 1988
Production: number of aircraft delivered, 53; on order, 4
Powerplant: two 1,700shp General Electric CT7-7A turboprops
Performance: maximum speed 174km/h (94kt); maximum cruising speed 446km/h (241kt) at 5,486m (18,000ft); range with maximum payload 842km (523 miles); range with maximum fuel 4,824km (3,015 miles)
Weights: empty 9,400kg (20,723lb); ramp 14,450kg (31,857lb); maximum take-off 14,400kg (31,747lb); maximum landing 14,200kg (31,306lb)
Dimensions: span 25.8m (84ft 6in); length 21.35m (70ft); height 8.17m (26ft 8in); wing area 59.1m² (636sq ft)
Seating capacity: 44
History: a joint venture between Spain and Indonesia, it follows on from the successful Casa 212-300, which Nusantara (formerly Nurtanio) assembled under licence. The CN-235 was delayed for more than a year owing to control ineffectiveness in the horizontal stabiliser.

The CN-235 hoping to build on the success of its forerunner

Cessna Model 208 Caravan 1

Country of origin: USA
First flight: December 1982
Entered airline service: 1985
Powerplant: one 600shp Pratt & Whitney (Canada) PT6A-114 turboprop
Performance: cruise speed 341km/h (184kt) at 3,050m (10,000ft); service ceiling 8,410m (27,600ft); range 2,326km (1,275 naut miles) with full payload
Weights: empty 1,724kg (3,800lb); maximum take-off 3,310kg (7,300lb)
Dimensions: span 15.88m (52.08ft); length 11.46m (37.58ft); wing area 25.96m² (279.4sq ft)
Seating capacity: 14
History: able to operate on sturdy wheeled or float landing gear, the 208 is a replacement for the Model 185 Skywagon. There are also two cargo variants, the Model 208A Cargomaster with an underfuselage cargo pannier and no fuselage windows, and the stretched version, 1.22m (4ft) longer Model 208B

The standard long-nosed Model 208 in flight

Cessna 402 Utiliner

Country of origin: USA
First flight: July 1962
Production: number built, 1,536
Powerplant: two Continental TS10-520-E flat-six piston engines, each rated at 300hp for take-off
Performance: maximum speed 420km/h (261mph) at 4,875m (16,000ft); maximum cruising speed 386km/h (240mph) at 6,096m (20,000ft); range 1,860-2,280km (1,156-1,417 miles)
Weights: empty operating 1,767kg (3,896lb); maximum take-off 2,857kg (6,300lb); maximum landing 2,812kg (6,200lb)
Dimensions: span 12.15m (39ft 10in); length 11.5m (36ft 1in); height 3.56m (11ft 8in); wing area 18.18m² (195.7sq ft)
Seating capacity: 10
History: began with the Cessna 411, of which over 300 were built by 1968, when it was replaced by the lighter Cessna 401. The 401, with accommodation for eight, first flew on 25 August 1965. The 402 was introduced along-side the 401, which gave way in 1971 to the 402B. The Model 402 had a quick-change interior for commuter passengers or freight.

The Model 402 was updated to the six/eight-seat Business-liner, while the 401 was phased out as early as 1972

Convair CV-440 Metropolitan

Country of origin: USA
First flight: October 1955
Production: 181 built; 22 in service
Powerplant: two 2,500hp Pratt & Whitney R-2800-CB16 or CB17 piston radials
Performance: maximum cruising speed 483km/h (300mph) at 3,962m (13,000ft); range with maximum payload 459km (285 miles), maximum fuel 3,106km (1,930 miles)
Weights: basic operating 15,110kg (33,314lb); maximum payload 5,820kg (12,836lb); maximum take-off 22,544kg (49,700lb)
Dimensions: span 32.12m (105ft 4in); length 24.84m (81ft 6in); height 8.59m (28ft 2in); wing area 85.5m² (920sq ft)
Seating capacity: 52
History: the CV-240 series was developed in the hope of producing a successor to the legendary Douglas DC-3, and although the type was good in every aspect, it failed to make a decisive impact when vast numbers of C-47s were released onto the civil market at the end of World War II. The CV-240 was followed by the more powerful CV-340 and then the CV-440, with high-density seating for up to 52 passengers.

An early Convair-240 of Pan American World Airways, capable of carrying 40 passengers with a
130 *crew of four*

de Havilland (Boeing) Canada DHC-6 Twin Otter Srs 300

Country of origin: Canada
First flight: May 1965
Powerplant: two 486-ekw (652eshp) Pratt & Whitney Aircraft of Canada PT6A-27 turboprops
Performance: maximum cruising speed 338km/h (210mph) at 3,050m (10,000ft); service ceiling 8,140m (26,700ft); range with 1,134kg (2,500lb) payload 1,297km (806 miles)
Weights: empty operating 3,363kg (7,415lb); maximum take-off 5,670kg (12,500lb)
Dimensions: span 19.81m (65ft); length 15.77m (51ft 9in); height 5.94m (19ft 6in); wing area 39.02m² (420sq ft)
Seating capacity: 20
History: production of the first five twin-engined STOL aircraft began in November 1964 and, because of the large commonality with the single-engined Otter, de Havilland was able to make a first flight on 20 May 1965. In Spring 1969, deliveries of the Srs 300 began.

Skis or floats can be fitted to the Twin Otter series, instead of the standard wheels of the fixed tricycle landing gear

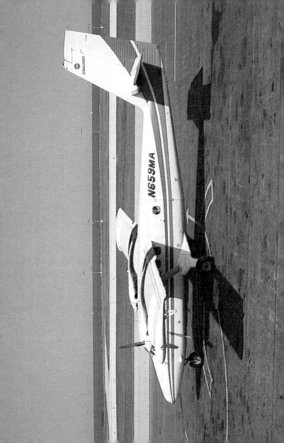

de Havilland (Boeing) Canada Dash 7

Country of origin: Canada
First flight: March 1975
Production: number built, 114; in airline service, 90
Powerplant: four 1,120shp Pratt & Whitney (VACL) PT6A-50 turboprops
Performance: maximum cruising speed 452km/h (281mph) at 4,570m (15,000ft); initial rate of climb 6.51m/sec (1,310ft/min); service ceiling 6,770m (22,200ft); range with maximum payload 1,504km (935 miles); range with maximum fuel 2,293km (1,425 miles)
Weights: operating empty 11,730kg (25,860lb); maximum payload 5,280kg (11,640lb); maximum take-off 19,504kg (43,000lb)
Dimensions: span 28.35m (93ft); length 24.5m (80ft 4in); height 8m (26ft 3in); wing area 79.9m² (860sq ft)
Seating capacity: 48-54
History: developed by de Havilland Canada in the 1970s, the Dash 7 is a rugged STOL airliner, able to seat up to 50 passengers, which has secured a major slice of the specialised market for which it was designed. The Dash 7 first entered service with Rocky Mountain Airway in February 1978.

The Dash-7 was quick to capture a large slice of the specialised market for which it was designed

de Havilland (Boeing) Canada Dash 8

Country of origin: Canada
First flight: June 1983
Production: number delivered 220; on order, 118
Powerplant: two 1,342kW (1,800shp) Pratt & Whitney Aircraft of Canada PW120 turboprops
Performance: maximum cruising speed 499km/h (310mph) at 4,570m (15,000ft); normal range with fuel reserves 1,056km (656 miles)
Weights: empty operating 9,793kg (21,590lb); maximum take-off 14,969kg (33,000lb)
Dimensions: span 25.9m (84ft 11.5in); length 22.25m (73ft); height 7.44m (24ft 5in); wing area 54.35m² (585sq ft)
Seating capacity: 36
History: designed as a commuter liner following the success of the Dash 7, the Dash 8 series 100 has been joined by a second variant, the series 300, which has a greater span and length to allow up to 56 passengers. The Dash 8 series 100 entered service with NorOntair in October 1984.

Air BC took delivery of eight Dash 8 Series 100s

Dornier Do228-201

Country of origin: West Germany
Production: 120 built; 100 in service
Powerplant: two 715shp Garrett 7PE 331-5 turboprops
Performance: maximum speed 148km/h (80kt); maximum cruising speed 424km/h (231kt) at 3,050m (10,000ft); range with maximum payload 1,112km (600 naut miles); range with maximum fuel 1,390km (750 naut miles)
Weights: empty operating 3,557kg (7,842lb); maximum take-off 5,980kg (13,183lb) maximum landing 5,700kg (12,676lb)
Dimensions: span 16.97m (55ft 8in); length 16.65m (54ft 4in); height 4.86m (15ft 8in); wing area 32m² (344sq ft)
Seating capacity: 19
History: a most distinctive aircraft with its drooped nose, tapered wingtips and a slope-sided fuselage, the 228 is also produced under licence in India by Hindustan Aeronautics, whose first production craft flew in February 1986, just prior to the 100th delivery from West Germany. An excellent airfield performance has meant that the 228 is taking over from the ageing Twin Otter as the 'difficult conditions' work-horse. The initial 100 series was a shorter 15-seat variant.

A Do228 commuter-liner, which utilises Dornier's patented TNT high-technology wing

Douglas DC-3

Country of origin: USA
First flight: July 1933
Production: 10,926 built; 290 in service
Powerplant: two 1,200hp Pratt & Whitney R-1830-92 Twin Wasp piston engines
Performance: maximum speed 346km/h (215mph); range with maximum payload 563km (350 miles); range with maximum fuel 2,430km (1,510 miles)
Weights: operating empty 8,030kg (17,720lb); maximum payload 3,000kg (6,600lb); maximum take-off 11,430kg (25,200lb)
Dimensions: span 28.96m (95ft); length 19.66m (64ft 6in); height 5.16m (16ft 11.5in); wing area 91.7m² (987sq ft)
Seating capacity: 24
History: the aircraft that changed history, first by opening the era of modern air travel in the mid-1930s, and then by becoming the mainstay of the Allies' air transport effort in World War II. Nearly 11,000 ware built in the USA, with a further 2,000 under licence in the USSR as the Lisunov Li-Z. The aircraft featured retractable landing gear, trailing edge flaps, and enclosed accommodation. Ordered by the US military as the C-47 Skytrain, supplied to the British under lend-lease, and named by them Dakota.

The immortal DC-3, the aircraft that's done everything and been everywhere

Douglas DC-4

Country of origin: USA
First flight: February 1942
Production: 1,242 built; 25 in service
Powerplant: four 1,450hp Pratt & Whitney R-2000-25D-13G Twin Wasp piston radials
Performance: maximum speed 426km/h (265mph); range with maximum payload 1,850km (1,150 miles); range with maximum fuel 3,510km (2,180 miles)
Weights: empty equipped 20,865kg (46,000lb); maximum payload 6,440kg (14,200lb); maximum take-off 33,112kg (73,000lb); maximum landing and maximum zero-fuel 28,860kg (63,500lb)
Dimensions: span 35.82m (117ft 6in); length 28.47m (93ft 5in); height 8.41m (27ft 7in); wing area 135.8m² (1,462sq ft)
Seating capacity: 42
History: the DC-4 was planned at the same time as the DC-3, and was to be a longer-range air transport with four engines, tricycle landing gear and greater capacity. Owing to the intervention of World War II, the production lines at Douglas were taken over by the military so that when the first DC-4A production aircraft flew on 14 February 1942, it was in the form of a military C-54 Skymaster, but American Overseas Airlines were able to take delivery in late 1945.

After World War II, many DC-4s
found their way onto the civil register

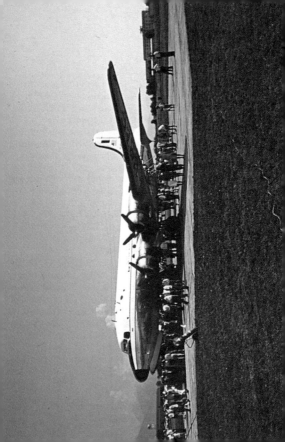

Douglas DC-6B

Country of origin: USA
First flight: February 1946
Production: number built, all DC-6 variants, 537; of DC-6B 288 were built; in service, 76
Powerplant: four 2,500hp Pratt & Whitney R-2800-CB17 piston radial engines
Performance: cruising speed 509km/h (316mph); range with maximum payload 4,828km (3,000 miles); range with maximum fuel 7,576km (4,720 miles)
Weights: maximum payload 11,143kg (24,565lb; maximum take-off 48,534kg (107,000lb)
Dimensions: span 35.81m (117ft 6in); length 32.2m (105ft 7in); height 8.92m (29ft 3in); wing area 135.9m² (1,463sq ft)
Seating capacity: basic 52
History: the first commercial order for 50 DC-6 aircraft was placed by American Airlines in 1944, with further orders from United soon after. Deliveries to both commenced in November 1946, with the first commercial service being flown on 27 April 1947. Scheduled flying time coast-to-coast eastbound was 10 hours, and 11 hours westbound. The DC-6B made its first flight on 2 February 1951, and was one of the best piston-engined airliners, having outstanding mechanical reliability.

One of the first DC-6 aircraft of
United, in late 1946

Douglas DC-7C

Country of origin: USA
Production: number built of all DC-7s, 338; of DC-7Cs, 121; number in airline service, 4
Powerplant: four 3,400hp Wright R3350-EA1 or EA4 piston radial engines
Performance: cruising speed 555km/h (345mph); service ceiling 6,615m (21,700ft); range with maximum payload 5,810km (3,610 miles); range with maximum fuel 9,077km (5,642 miles)
Weights: basic operating 36,287kg (80,000lb); maximum payload 9,752 kg (21,500lb); maximum take-off 64,865kg (143,000lb)
Dimensions: span 38.8m (127ft 6in); length 34.23m (112ft 3in); height 9.65m (31ft 8in); wing area 152m² (1,637sq ft)
Seating capacity: 105
History: the first DC-7 flight was made on 18 May 1953. The final development, and the last piston-engined commercial aircraft to be built by Douglas, was the DC-7C. It entered service with Pan American on 1 June 1956, and 12 other airlines including BOAC also placed orders. SAS flew the first 'over the pole' Europe-Far East service on 24 February 1957.

A DC-7B of National, superceded by the DC-7C; the DC-7B was capable of transcontinental routes with additional fuel capacity

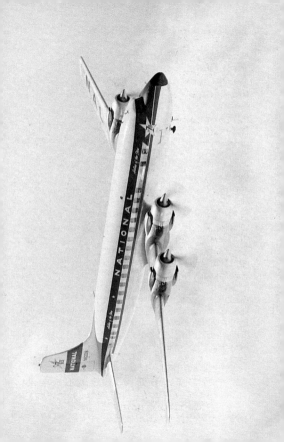

EMBRAER EMB-110 P-2

Country of origin: Brazil
First flight: October 1968
Powerplant: two 559kW (750shp) Pratt & Whitney Aircraft of Canada PT6A-34 turboprops
Performance: maximum cruising speed 414km/h (257mph) at 2,440m (8,000ft); economic cruising speed 330km/h (208mph) at 3,050m (10,000ft); service ceiling 6,860m (22,500ft); range with fuel reserves 2,000km (1,243 miles)
Weights: empty equipped 3,555kg (7,837lb); maximum take-off 5,670kg (12,500lb)
Dimensions: span 15.55m (50ft 3.5in); length 15.1m (49ft 6.5in); height 4.92m (16ft 1.75in); wing area 29.1m² (313.23sq ft)
Seating capacity: 21
History: the first production aircraft entered service with the Brazilian Air Force in 1972 with Transbrazil and VASP taking their deliveries in 1973. The EMB-110 Bandeirante was used as a feeder liner to replace Douglas DC-3s and has a seating capacity of 15. Notable variants include the 18-passenger, three-abreast EMB-110P, which entered service in 1976 with TABA. The EMB-110 P-2 had a fuselage stretched by 0.84m (2ft 9in), as did the all-cargo EMB-110K-1 version.

The Empresa Brasileira de Aeronautico SA was created in 1969

EMBRAER EMB-120 Brasilia

Country of origin: Brazil
First flight: July 1983
Production: number of aircraft delivered, 128; on order, 124
Powerplant: two 1,590shp Pratt & Whitney AC PW115 turboprops
Performance: maximum speed 290km/h (108kt); maximum cruising speed 584km/h (294kt) at 6,096m (20,000ft); range with maximum fuel 3,263km (1,760 naut miles)
Weights: empty 6,835kg (15,068lb); maximum take-off 10,800kg (23,810lb); maximum landing 10,550kg (23,250lb)
Dimensions: span 19.78m (64ft 9in); length 20m (65ft 6in); height 6.35m (20ft 8in); wing area 38.03m² (409sq ft)
Seating capacity: 30
History: the EMB-120 obtained certification in the USA in July 1985, and entered service the following month with Atlantic Southeast Airlines of Atlanta, whose initial order was for 10 aircraft. European operation commenced in January 1986 with the West German operator DLT.

Atlantic Southeast Airlines uses its Brasilias for its Delta Connection service for Delta Airlines

EMBRAER EMB-121 Xinga

Country of origin: Brazil
First flight: October 1976
Powerplant: two Pratt & Whitney (Canada) PT6A-28 turboprops, each rated at 680shp for take-off
Performance: maximum cruising speed 450km/h (280mph) at 3,353m (11,000ft); initial rate of climb 7.11m/sec (1,400ft/min); service ceiling 7,925m (26,000ft); maximum range 2,352km (1,462 miles) with payload of 610kg (1,340lb)
Weights: empty operating 3,500kg (7,716lb); maximum take-off 5,670kg (12,500lb); maximum landing 5,340kg (11,773lb)
Dimensions: span 14.45m (47ft 5in); length 12.25m (40ft 2.25in); height 4.74m (15ft 6.5in); wing area 27.5m² (296sq ft)
Seating capacity: 6
History: first deliveries were in 1978, with the first commercial deliveries in June 1979. A derivative of the Embraer Bandeirante, the Xinga is aimed at the executive market. It has a circular-section pressurised fuselage that is shorter than that of the Bandeirante, a T-tail, more powerful engines and a shorter wingspan.

The Brazilian-built Xingu is a compact, yet highly sophisticated business jet

152

Fokker F.27 Friendship Mk 200

Country of origin: Netherlands
First flight: November 1955
Production: number built, 581; in airline service, 314
Powerplant: two 2,105eshp Rolls-Royce Dart 528 or 528-7E or 2,230eshp Dart 532-7 turboprops
Performance: cruising speed 486km/h (302mph); initial rate of climb 7.5m/sec (1,475ft/min); service ceiling 9,000m (29,500ft); range with maximum payload 2,070km (1,285 miles); range with maximum fuel 2,211km (1,374 miles)
Weights: empty 10,295kg (22,696lb); operating empty 11,159kg (24,600lb); maximum payload 4,690kg (10,340lb); maximum take-off 20,410kg (45,000lb)
Dimensions: span 29m (95ft 2in); length 23.56m (77ft 3.5in); height 8.51m (27ft 11in); wing area 70m² (753.5sq ft)
Seating capacity: 36
History: the first production aircraft flew on 23 March 1958, these being similar to a second prototype and powered by Dart 511 engines. The F.27 Friendship became the best-selling turboprop transport, outside the USSR, when coupled with the production of the stretched version, Fairchild FH-227, and the three basic versions.

Fokker F.50

Country of origin: Netherlands
First flight: December 1985
Production: number of aircraft delivered, 87; on order, 40
Powerplant: two Pratt & Whitney PW124 turboprops; take-off power 2,160shp
Performance: maximum cruising speed 515km/h (278kt) at 6,400m (21,000ft); range with maximum payload 2,091km (1,129 naut miles); range with maximum fuel 4,119km (2,224 naut miles)
Weights: empty 12,633kg (27,850lb); maximum take-off 20,820kg (45,900lb); maximum landing 18,990kg (41,865lb)
Dimensions: span 29m (95ft 1.5in); length 25.25m (82ft 8in); height 8.6m (28ft 6in); wing area 70m² (754sq ft)
Seating capacity: 50
History: launched together with the Fokker 100 programme at the end of 1983, the F.50 is Fokker's replacement for the F.27 Friendship, which commenced operations in 1958. The F.50 retains the same fuselage length. It entered service with Ansett Transport Industries in 1987.

Eurolink relies heavily on the F.50 for its feeder routes in central
Europe

GAF Nomad N22

Country of origin: Australia
First flight: July 1971
Powerplant: two Allison 250-B17B turboprops, each rated at 400shp for take-off
Performance: normal cruising speed 311km/h (193mph); initial rate of climb 7.4m/sec (1,460ft/min); service ceiling 6,860m (22,500ft); maximum range 1,352km (840 miles)
Weights: operating empty 2,116kg (4,666lb); maximum take-off 3,855kg (8,500lb)
Dimensions: span 16.46m (54ft); length 12.56m (41ft 2.5in); height 5.52m (18ft 1.5in); wing area 30.1m² (324sq ft)
Seating capacity: 12
History: the Nomad entered service on 18 December 1975 with Aero Pelican. The fuselage is almost square in cross-section and incorporates large side-loading doors. A stretched fuselage version, 1.14m (3ft 9in) longer, designated N24, entered service in 1976, with additional seating for a further three passengers.

The Nomad has proved rugged and reliable in use

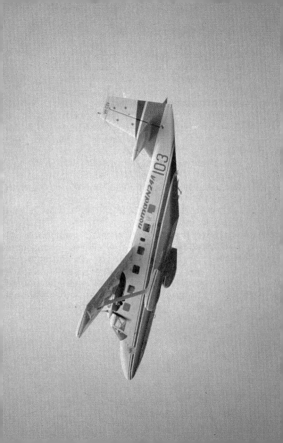

Grumman Gulfstream 1-C

Country of origin: USA
Production: number built, 200
Powerplant: two Rolls-Royce Dart RD27 Mk 529-8X
Performance: maximum cruising speed 560km/h (348mph); initial rate of climb 9.6m/sec (1,900ft/min); service ceiling 10,240m (33,600ft); range with maximum fuel 4,058km (2,540 miles)
Weights: empty operating 11,295kg (24,850lb); maximum take-off 16,363kg (36,000lb); maximum landing 15,584kg (34,285lb)
Dimensions: span 23.92m (78ft 6in); length 22.96m (75ft 4in); height 7.01m (23ft); wing area 56.7m² (610.3sq ft)
Seating capacity: 37
History: originating in 1956 as a large executive aircraft, the first flight was on 14 August 1958, and deliveries commenced in 1959. Production of the 10-seat model ended in February 1969, when it gave way to the Gulfstream II. In 1979, Gulfstream American started production on a 32-38-seat commuter version, and conversions are now available with a fuselage lengthened by 3.25m (10ft 8in).

A Gulfstream 1 at Berlin in 1988; a TC-4 crew trainer variant was also produced for the USA Navy

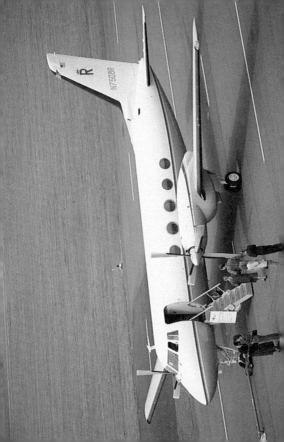

Handley Page Herald 200

Country of origin: UK
First flight: August 1955
Production: number built, 50; in service, 6
Powerplant: two 2,105ehp Rolls-Royce Dart 527 turboprops
Performance: maximum cruising speed 441km/h (274mph) at 4,572m (15,000ft); best economy cruise 426km/h (265mph) at 7,010m (23,000ft); initial rate of climb 9.1m/sec (1,805ft/min); service ceiling 8,504m (27,900ft); range with maximum payload 1,786km (1,110 miles); range with maximum fuel 2,607km (1,620 miles)
Weights: operating empty 11,700kg (25,800lb); maximum payload 5,100kg (11,242lb); maximum take-off 19,505kg (43,000lb)
Dimensions: span 28.88m (94ft 9in); length 23.01m (75ft 6in); height 7.34m (24ft 1in); wing area 82.3m² (888sq ft)
Seating capacity: 44
History: originally designed as a piston-engined feeder-line aircraft to seat 44 passengers, the Herald finally entered production with Dart turboprops. The first production Srs 200 flew on 13 December 1961, and entered service with Jersey Airlines the following month.

The last of the Handley Page Heralds will soon be withdrawn from service

Ilyushin Il-18D

Country of origin: USSR
First flight: July 1955
Production: number built, 565; in airline service, 125+
Powerplant: four Ivchenko A1-20 M turboprops, each rated at 4,250ehp
Performance: maximum cruising speed at maximum take-off weight 675km/h (419mph); range with maximum payload and one hour reserve 3,700km (2,300 miles); range with maximum fuel and one hour reserve 6,500km (4,040 miles)
Weights: empty equipped (90-seater) 35,000kg (77,160lb); maximum take-off 64,000kg (141,000lb)
Dimensions: span 37.4m (122ft 8.5in); length 35.9m (117ft 9in); height 10.17m (33ft 4in); wing area 140m² (1,507sq ft)
Seating capacity: 110
History: the airliner entered service with Aeroflot on 20 April 1959. It was originally produced as the Il-18A with either Kuznetsov NK-4 or Ivchenko AI-20K engines and seating capacity of 75, but then the Il-18B was introduced with an increased seating capacity of 84 and the Ivchenko engines became standard. In 1961 the 89-100-passenger variant Il-18V was introduced, and in 1965 the Il-18I entered service.

The Il-18 was the USSR's equivalent of the Lockheed Electra

LET L-410A Turbolet

Country of origin: Czechoslovakia
First flight: April 1975
Production: number produced, 650+
Powerplant: two 715eshp Pratt & Whitney (VACL) PT6A-27 turboprops
Performance: maximum cruising speed 370km/h (230mph) at 3,000m (9,840ft); best economy cruise 360km/h (224mph); initial rate of climb 8.2m/sec (1,610ft/min); service ceiling 7,100m (23,300ft); range with maximum payload 300km (186 miles); range with maximum fuel 1,300km (807 miles)
Weights: operating empty 3,100kg (6,834lb); maximum take-off 5,700kg (12,566lb); maximum landing 5,500kg (12,125lb)
Dimensions: span 17.48m (57ft 4.5in); length 13.61m (44ft 7.75in); height 5.65m (18ft 6.5in); wing area 32.86m² (353.7sq ft)
Seating capacity: 15
History: developed by the Czechoslovakian National Aircraft Industry, the L-410 was to have been powered by Czech-built M-601 engines, but these were not ready in time and the prototype flew with Pratt & Whitney PT6A-27 engines.

Mass-produced, and used extensively throughout Czechoslovakia

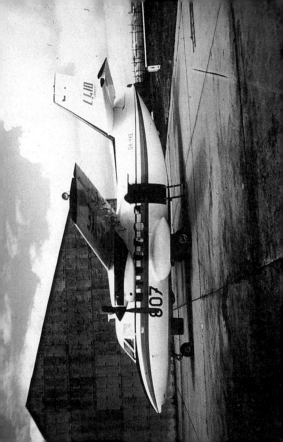

Lockheed Electra L-188A

Country of origin: USA
First flight: December 1967
Production: 170 built; 70 in service
Powerplant: four 3,750ehp Allison 501-D13A turboprops
Performance: maximum cruising speed 652km/h (405mph) at 6,700m (22,000ft); best economy cruise 602km/h (374mph); initial rate of climb 8.5m/sec (1,670ft/min); service ceiling 8,230m (27,000ft); range with maximum payload 3,540km (2,200 miles); range with maximum fuel 4,023km (2,500 miles)
Weights: basic operating 27,895kg (61,500lb); maximum payload 10,350kg (22,825lb); maximum take-off 52,664kg (116,000lb)
Dimensions: span 30.18m (99ft); length 31.81m (104ft 6in); height 10m (32ft 10in); wing area 120.8m² (1,300sq ft)
Seating capacity: 100
History: the Electra entered service with Eastern on 12 January 1959 and with American 11 days later. It was to be the only US-designed and produced turboprop to operate regular services. An advanced type with all-metal construction, retractable landing gear and other advanced features.

The Lockheed Electra was a short to medium-range transport, developed for the USA domestic market

168

Lockheed L-100-3-Hercules

Country of origin: USA
First flight: August 1970
Production: number built (civil version), 68; in airline service, 43
Powerplant: four 4,508eshp Allison 501-D22A turboprops
Performance: maximum cruising speed 607km/h (377mph); initial rate of climb 9.65m/sec (1,900ft/min); range with maximum payload 3,425km (2,130 miles); range with maximum fuel 7,630km (4,740 miles)
Weights: operating empty 32,386kg (71,400lb); maximum payload 23,315kg (51,400lb); maximum take-off 70,308kg (155,000lb)
Dimensions: span 40.41m (132ft 7in); length 34.35m (112ft 8.5in); height 11.66m (38ft 3in); wing area 162.12m² (1,745sq ft)
History: the civilian version, the L-100-20, was a stretched-fuselage variant, 2.54m (8ft 3in) longer, of the basic military C-130. The L-100-30 was a further fuselage stretch of 2.03m (6ft 6.75in). The type pioneered the modern airlifter layout with high wing, capacious fuselage with a rectangular-section hold, and an integral rear ramp/door that allows the straight-in loading/unloading of bulky items under the upswept tail.

The world's major turboprop tactical transport

Mitsubishi Mu-2

Country of origin: Japan
First flight: September 1963
Powerplant: two Garrett-AiResearch TPE331-6-251M turboprops, each rated at 724ehp for take-off
Performance: maximum cruising speed 589km/h (365mph); initial rate of climb 14.5m/sec (2,840ft/min); service ceiling 9,815m (32,200ft); maximum range 2,705km (1,680 miles)
Weights: empty operating 3,113kg (6,864lb); maximum take-off 4,750kg (10,470lb); maximum landing 4,515kg (9,955lb)
Dimensions: span 11.94m (39ft 2in); length 10.13m (33ft 3in); height 3.94m (12ft 11in); wing area 16.55m² (178sq ft)
Seating capacity: 7
History: the first production craft, powered by the TPE 331-6 engines, flew on 11 March 1965. Following its success, the stretched-fuselage Mu-2G version capable of carrying an additional two passengers was produced and first flew on 10 January 1969.

The Mu-2 was the forerunner of the Mu-300 business jet, and which Mitsubishi subsequently sold off to Beech

NAMC YS-11A

Country of origin: Japan
First flight: August 1962
Production: 182 built; 105 in service
Powerplant: two 3,060hp Rolls-Royce Dart
542-10K turboprops
Performance: maximum cruising speed at
4,575m (15,000ft) 469km/h (291mph); range
with maximum payload 1,090km (680 miles);
range with maximum fuel 3,215km (2,000
miles)
Weights: operating empty 15,419kg
(33,993lb); maximum payload 6,581kg
(14,508lb); maximum take-off 24,500kg
(54,010lb)
Dimensions: span 32m (104ft 11.75in); length
26.3m (86ft 3.5in); height 8.98m (29ft 5.5in);
wing area 94.8m² (1,020.4sq ft)
Seating capacity: 60
History: the first Japanese-designed and produced commercial aircraft to enter production,
the NAMC YS-11 short-to-medium range airliner entered service with Toa Airlines (now
TDA) in April 1965. The YS-11A was produced
specifically for north America, and deliveries to
Piedmont Aviation were made in 1968. Production ceased in 1973, and NAMC went into liqui-
dation.

*The NAMC YS-11A started well but
ran out of customers in a highly
competitive market*

Pilatus Britten-Norman Islander BN-2A-2

Country of origin: UK
First flight: June 1965
Production: number built, 1,070
Powerplant: two 260hp Avro Lycoming 0-540-E4C5 piston engines
Performance: maximum speed 290km/h (180mph); typical cruise 270km/h (168mph) at 2,750m (9,000ft); initial rate of climb 6.35m/sec (1,250ft/min); service ceiling 5,013m (10,400ft); range at typical speed 1,287km (800 miles)
Weights: basic operating 1,695kg (3,738lb); maximum take-off 2,857kg (6,300lb)
Dimensions: span 14.94m (49ft); length 10.86m (35ft 7.75in); height 4.18m (13ft 8.75in); wing area 30.19m² (325sq ft)
Seating capacity: 9
History: the first production craft flew on 24 April 1967; the Islander entered service on 13 August 1967 with Glosair, and two days later with Loganair. It was designed as a simple feeder-liner for operators in remote areas and has a payload capacity of up to 755kg (1,665lb).

An Allison 250 turboprop-powered
PBN Islander BN-2T

Pilatus Britten-Norman Trislander

Country of origin: UK
First flight: September 1970
Powerplant: three 260 Lycoming O-540-E4C5 piston engines
Performance: maximum cruising speed 283km/h (176mph) at 1,988m (6,500ft); typical cruise 280km/h (174mph) at 2,750m (9,000ft); initial rate of climb 4.98m/sec (980ft/min); service ceiling 4,010m (13,150ft); range with maximum payload 338km (210 miles); range with maximum fuel 1,384km (860 miles)
Weights: basic operating 2,800kg (6,178lb); maximum payload 1,610kg (3,550lb) maximum take-off 4,536kg (10,000lb)
Dimensions: span 16.15m (53ft); length 13.34m (43ft 9in); length with extended nose 14.48m (47ft 6in); height 4.11m (13ft 5.75in); wing area 31.25m² (337sq ft)
Seating capacity: 17
History: an evolution from the Islander, the Trislander has considerable commonality including the fuselage cross-section, mainplane and powerplant. Differences include the stretched fuselage and a third engine, which is located in the tail fin. Deliveries began on 29 June 1971, and the first flight of the Trislander with the stretched fuselage was on 18 August 1974.

Looking slightly unwieldy, but highly effective

Piper PA-31T Cheyenne II

Country of origin: USA
Powerplant: two Pratt & Whitney (Canada) PT6A-28 turboprops, each rated at 620eshp for take-off
Performance: maximum cruising speed 525km/h (326mph) at 3,355m (11,000ft); initial rate of climb 14.2m/sec (2,800ft/min); service ceiling 8,840m (29,000ft); maximum range 2,080-2,739km (1,621-1,702 miles)
Weights: empty operating 2,209kg (4,870lb); maximum take-off and landing 4,082kg (9,000lb)
Dimensions: span 13.01m (42ft 8.25in); length 10.57m (34ft 8in); height 3.89m (12ft 9in); wing area 21.3m² (229sq ft)
Seating capacity: 6
History: a turboprop version of the Navajo, the Cheyenne first flew on 20 August 1969 and entered service in 1974. It was Piper's first turbine- engined business aircraft. The first production aircraft, designated Cheyenne II, flew on 22 October 1973. The Cheyenne I was introduced in 1977 as a low-cost variant powered by Pratt & Whitney PT6A-11 engines.

Various upgrades and extensions have finally resulted in the Cheyenne IV, with Garrett TPE-331-14A/B turboprops

Saab SF 340

Country of origin: Sweden
First flight: January 1983
Production: number of aircraft delivered, 184; on order, 143
Powerplant: two 1,735shp General Electric CT7-5A1 turboprops
Performance: maximum speed 206km/h (111kt); maximum cruising speed 500km/h (270kt) at 4,572m (15,000ft); range with maximum payload 1,191km (643 miles); range with maximum fuel 3,332km (1,798 miles)
Weights: empty operating 7,899kg (17,415lb); maximum take-off 12,372kg (27,275lb); maximum landing 12,020kg (26,500lb)
Dimensions: span 21.44m (70ft 4in); length 19.42m (67ft 9in); height 6.87m (22ft 6in); wing area 41.81m² (450sq ft)
Seating capacity: 35
History: a joint development between Saab and Fairchild, announced in 1980, the 340 was intended specifically for the short-haul commuter market, and designed to be easily maintained and operated. In 1985 Fairchild withdrew and Saab took over all financial obligations, retaining Fairchild as a subcontractor until early 1987. The 340 entered service with Crossair of Switzerland in 1984.

The Saab 340 is of the all-metal type of construction, with selective use
182 *of composite materials*

Shorts Skyvan

Country of origin: UK
First flight: October 1963
Powerplant: two Garrett-AiResearch TPE331-201 turboprops, each rated at 715shp for take-off
Performance: maximum cruising speed 327km/h (203mph); initial rate of climb 8.3m/sec (1,640ft/min); service ceiling 6,858m (22,500ft); range up to 1,115km (694 miles); range with 1,814kg (4,000lb) of freight 300km (187 miles)
Weights: basic operating 3,331kg (7,344lb); maximum payload 2,086kg (4,600lb); maximum take-off 5,670kg (12,500lb)
Dimensions: span 19.79m (64ft 11in); length 12.21m (40ft 1in); height 4.6m (15ft1in); wing area 34.65m² (373sq ft)
Seating capacity: 19
History: the Skyvan Srs 2 entered service in 1966, and the Srs 3 in 1968, in 1970 obtaining its UK airworthiness certificate for STOL operations. Several military variants have been produced, in addition to the Skyliner version of the Skyvan Srs 3, which can accommodate up to 22 passengers.

The successful Sh.7 Skyvan,
forerunner of the Shorts 330

Shorts 330

Country of origin: UK
First flight: August 1974
Production: number delivered, 75; on order, 55
Powerplant: two 1,120shp Pratt & Whitney (UACL) PT6A-45 turboprops
Performance: maximum cruising speed 367km/h (228mph) at 3,050m (10,000ft); long-range cruise 296km/h (184mph); initial rate of climb 6.5m/sec (1,280ft/min); range with maximum payload 805km (500 miles) with 30 passengers at long-range cruise speed and with 20 passengers at long-range cruise speed 1,400km (870 miles)
Weights: empty equipped 5,753kg (12,685lb); design maximum payload 3,400kg (7,500lb); maximum take-off 9,979kg (22,000lb)
Dimensions: span 22.78m (74ft 9in); length 17.69m (58ft 0.5in); height 4.78m (15ft 8in); wing area 42.1m² (453sq ft)
Seating capacity: 30
History: the 330 is a derivative of the Skyvan STOL utility transport. First orders were placed by Command Airways of the USA and Time Air of Canada, and the 330 entered service with Time Air on 24 August 1976. A rear-loading variant designated UTT (Utility Tactical Transport) is used by the USAF in Europe, and this includes a strengthened floor and inward-opening rear cabin doors for paradropping.

Shorts 360 Advanced

Country of origin: UK
First flight: August 1982
Production: number delivered, 179; on order, 2
Powerplant: two 1,424shp PWAC PT6A-65AR turboprops
Performance: maximum speed 195km/h (105kt); maximum cruising speed 393km/h (212kt) at 3,050m (10,000ft); range with maximum payload 417km (225 naut miles); range with maximum fuel 1,596km (861 naut miles)
Weights: maximum take-off 11,999kg (26,453lb); maximum landing 11,839kg (26,100lb)
Dimensions: span 22.78m (74ft 9in); length 21.58m (70ft 8in); height 7.21m (23ft 7in); wing area 40.1m² (453sq ft)
Seating capacity: 36
History: larger than the Shorts 330, the 360 retains the high wing and nose, and a conventional single tail in place of the twin tail of the 330. The first delivery was to Suburban Airlines of Reading, Pennsylvania in November 1982, and the 360 Advanced entered service early in 1986 with Thai Airways.

The 360-300 used a slightly lower-rated engine then the 360 Advanced

Index

Piston engined